The Seine

Great Rivers of the World

The Seine

Anthony Glyn

G. P. PUTNAM'S SONS
NEW YORK

FIRST AMERICAN EDITION 1967

© 1966 by Anthony Glyn

Library of Congress Catalog Card Number: 67-23014

PRINTED IN THE UNITED STATES OF AMERICA

Contents

Illustrations

(between pages 84 and 85)

Acknowledgements

The following illustrations for this volume were provided by the author: figures 1, 9, 10 and 18.

The author and publishers are grateful to the following for providing illustrations: Almasy, figures 13, 15, 24, 25, 26, 30, 31 and 33; British Museum, figures 27, 28 and 29; Yvan Christ, figure 19; French Government Tourist Office, figures 14 (Ina Bandy), 8 (Boudot-Lamotte), 20 (Marcel Louchet), and 34 (Lucien Vignier); Giraudon, figure 16; Gilbert Houel, figure 17; A. F. Kersting, figure 32; Edition "La Sequana", figure 4; Foto Marburg, figure 21; Musée Archéologique de Dijon, figure 2; J. Richard, figure 11; Roger-Viollet, figures 22, 23 and 35; Edwin Smith, figure 12.

Map drawn by Audrey Frew.

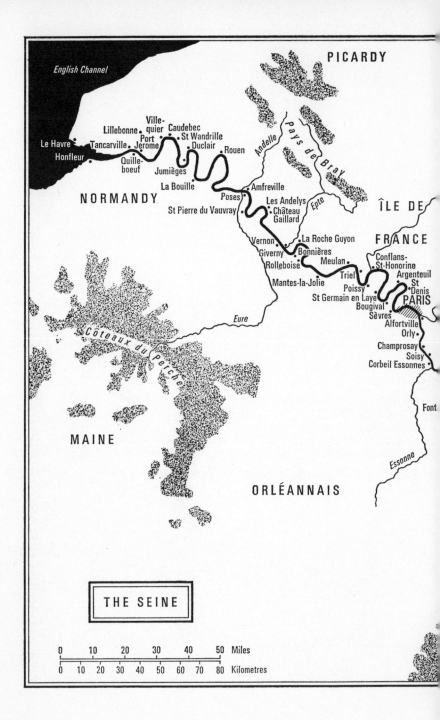

THE SEINE

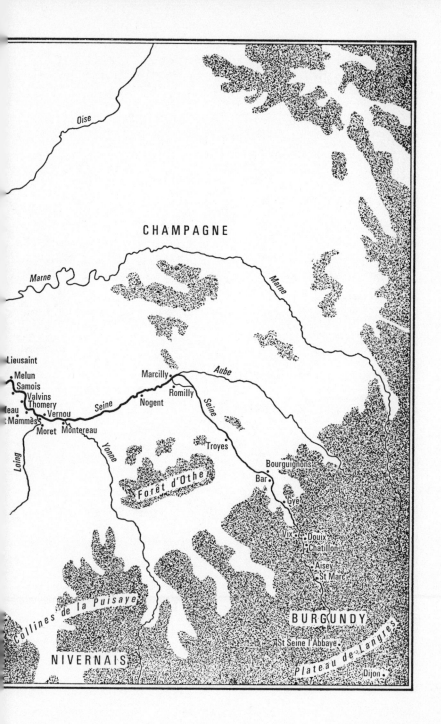

Introduction

I have the good fortune to live in the middle of the Seine, on the smaller of the two Paris islands, the Île Saint-Louis. The Seine is always just beyond my doorstep, I see it every day. It dominates my life, just as it dominates the life of the island. It is always there, thick, grey-green or black, a barrier against the hubbub beyond, an astounding slash of silence across the noisy city.

Sometimes, for days on end, I do not leave the island. There is no need, for the Île Saint-Louis is a self-contained community with its own shops and cafés. I stand for hours on the quays watching the river, the fishermen, the bâteaux-mouches, the barges, the patterns of bridges and trees and water. When I want to go to a post office, a bank, a métro station, the stores of the Boulevard Haussmann or the cafés of St Germain-des-Prés, I have to cross to the mainland. The Pont Sully is perhaps the ugliest bridge in Paris, but it is better to cross by an ugly bridge and look at a beautiful one than the other way round, and the views from the Pont Sully are the finest in the city. From the northern arch, joining the island to the right bank, I look upstream to the Pont Marie, one of the prettiest of Paris bridges, and the tower of Saint-Gervais. From the southern arch, which joins the island to the left bank, I can see Notre Dame rising above its chestnuts. The conductors of the No. 86 buses have learnt not to try to clip my ticket until we are on to the mainland and have turned on to the Quai de la Tournelle.

The Seine is a very placid river. High water or low, its flow is barely perceptible. Indeed, it often seems more like an attenuated lake, hundreds of miles long, a hundred yards wide. If you stand and stare at a floating leaf, it is amazing how slowly it moves towards Le Havre. Even more surprising are the occasions when it floats away in the opposite direction towards Burgundy and the Côte d'Or. Indeed, one of the curious things about the river is that, as often as not, it seems to be flowing upstream.

But if the Seine varies little, the scenery changes spectacularly through the day and the year. Winter nights with the river mist blotting everything out, though it will be clear and starry at the Bastille or the Panthéon; and hidden in the mist, in an orange glow, three clochards huddled round a fire by the Pont Sully, frying eggs. Dog days with the river bright blue with reflected sky and the tip of the island covered with bare torsos lying on newspapers. Autumn mornings with the trees turned, and the sun breaking through the mist. Spring days with the sky above full of Monet's light. Midsummer days with the river and island powdered with cottonseed from the poplars. Summer nights with the great trees and the Pont Marie and the buildings floodlit, and the shimmer of the lights on the mainland. If, like me, you have a passion for the shine of lights across water, the Île Saint-Louis is a good place to be. In the pathways of reflected light, if you look carefully, you will see the river fizzing like champagne.

Few rivers in the world are as thick in overtones as the Seine, and these overtones are as much part of the river as the actual water, the notes of the chord above the ground bass. Historic overtones: the cathedrals, palaces, churches, castles, battlefields. Or romantic: bridges, loving couples, fishermen, bookstalls, barges. Or artistic: Monet and Sisley, Mallarmé and Baudelaire. Or practical: traffic, pollution, suicides, generating plants. But the basic quality from which everything else derives, the undertone beneath the overtones, is unexpected and elusive and does not reveal itself in Paris, but at the source.

Holiness.

Part One: Upstream

1

Like the Jordan, the Ganges, the Rhine, the Seine is a holy river. In a hidden, wooded valley of the Côte d'Or, some twenty miles north of Dijon, on the watershed between northern and Mediterranean France, the Seine rises, and there the worship of the goddess Sequana was celebrated from earliest times. All springs tend to have their cults, of course, but the adoration of Sequana seems to have been something quite exceptional. Originally there was a wood and clay building on the site, but it was in the first century AD, under the Romans, that the cult really began to grow.

Two successive temples, each larger than the last, were built on the site. The second one was probably unique in France and the archaeological discoveries of September 1963 allow us to catch a glimpse of just how imposing it was. According to the archaeologist Jules Toutain, it was fifty-seven metres long and eighteen metres wide and in the centre sprang one of the several sources of the river. It ran in a small trench covered with flag-stones, through a colonnaded hall. Leading off the hall was the shrine of Sequana herself, and beside the hall were chapels where priests received the offerings of the faithful.

But the heart of the sanctuary was a little further downstream, where all the sources of the Seine joined. There was the bathing-pool, sixty metres long, and for three centuries pilgrims came there from all over France to worship the goddess and bathe in the holy water. In the words of a carefully anonymous French writer, 'Well before the rise of Christianity, well before the great modern pilgrimages – and perhaps the origin of all the beliefs which are today centred on Lourdes – we find the temple of Sequana'.

Indeed, the similarity to Lourdes is remarkable. The Seine also contained the gift of miraculous healing, and the sick and the crippled journeyed there from the Channel and Mediterranean coasts by horse, carriage or on foot, to be healed. Artists and artisans set up their booths beside the temple to sell votive offerings to the pilgrims. The rich could order statuettes of themselves, in stone or bronze, showing the exact details of their illnesses. The less well-to-do had to make do with wood or clay or with metal plaques, crudely stamped with the outline of the infected organ, and suitably gilded or silvered. Hundreds of these offerings have been recovered, the latest in September 1963, and they show clearly both the advanced and, despite the Roman occupation, the Celtic nature of the local art; and also the hideously modern diseases from which the Gauls suffered.

The offering made and accepted by the priests, the pilgrims went to bathe in the pool, remaining there for days on end, throwing in rings, coins and jewels to accelerate the cure. Apart from the pilgrims and the residents, many others passed that way to see the famous temple and to meet their friends. The valley must have been a hive of activity, very different from the desolation today.

It all came abruptly to an end in the third century AD. The smashing of the temple has been attributed to Christian missionaries, but this does not seem likely. For one thing it was too early, and for another Christian practice was to convert shrines rather than destroy them. It seems more probable that it was the work of a wandering tribe from Germany, possibly the advance guard of the Burgundians, whose main invasion was to follow so soon after.

The priests and artisans had warning of their coming; time to bury the statue of Sequana and the votive statuettes. Then they took to the woods while the shrine was desecrated and destroyed. Sequana herself was discovered recently and is now in the archaeological museum at Dijon. It is a graceful statue, some eighteen inches high, of a slender sympathetic girl, wearing Greek robes and a crown, holding out her hands in welcome. She stands in a small boat, whose prow is the head of a bird holding in its mouth a fruit, possibly a pomegranate.

She was undamaged, but her reign as a goddess was over. The cult of her river, however, went on, secretly, in the woods beside the source.

2

It is not easy to convey the atmosphere of that place, the feeling of uneasiness that still persists, of pagan cults and secret persecuted worship. The valley is remote, lonely, hidden, claustrophobic. On either side the hills rise steeply, thickly wooded, shutting out the usual wide French horizons. On the east side are some springs, sources of the Seine, which run down through the wood, through the shrine of Sequana into the sacred pool. On the other side is a small winding road, the only access, and above it another wooded hill. It was a grey end-of-summer day when I saw it, and the place seemed more lost than it must usually seem.

At the bottom of the valley are the trickling river, small fields, goats, fences, a hut and some spades. There is only one inhabited building, the Café Sequana. The temple itself is a wilderness of archaeological rubble, haphazard masonry, wire, mounds of earth, stagnant puddles, for archaeologists do not usually feel the call to tidy up before they leave.

The principal source, however, is not up the eastern hillside, but a hundred yards up the valley. The ground here is owned by the city of Paris and there, under a gloomy clump of evergreens, Napoleon III, or more exactly Haussmann, built a monument to Sequana and to the greater glory of Paris's river. It is a typically French folly such as you might find in any public garden: a large artificial grotto, a pool, a water-nymph (by Jouffroy, a local sculptor) reclining on a rock in the middle. The Seine bubbles out into the pool at the nymph's feet through a sort of sink-grating; from the pool it passes through a pipe under the path, and trickles away through the field, just four inches wide. It passes under the first of its many bridges, a brick bridge carrying a path, and disappears into the ruins of the temple and the bathing pool, the first few yards of its long journey to the sea.

Haussmann's grotto has been attacked for its modernity and romanticism. It is, of course, right out of key with its ancient site.

Jouffroy's nymph, naked except for a bunch of grapes, nicely rounded, eagerly awaiting seduction, is centuries away both in time and spirit from the chaste, robed, flat-chested goddess in the Dijon museum. But, all the same, I am grateful to Haussmann. For one thing, the principal source is honoured and marked and focused in a way that says 'Paris' as clearly as if it were written in neon. For another, the archaeologists, to their great annoyance, have been prevented from turning the chief source into another bombed-site. And the water-nymph, in her own right, is charming and typically French.

'How Burgundian,' I remarked to Jean-Paul, my driver, 'to show a water-goddess holding a bunch of grapes.'

He pointed at his face. 'That is why I have a red nose,' he commented.

I took the hint and suggested we move downstream to the Café Sequana. There he unexpectedly asked for Cointreau rather than Burgundy. He explained that it was better for the health. Did liqueurs, I wondered, have less impact on the appearance of the nasal organs?

I talked to Madame la patronne. Yes, there were few people here today, she agreed, but earlier in the summer it was very different. There were dozens of visitors a day, hundreds, from Paris, Rouen, Le Havre, coming to visit the source of their river. There were others too, she said, Belgians, Dutch, English, but it was mostly the French from the river.

I left Jean-Paul and wandered away through the fields. Below the café was Madame's bucket and scrubbing-board, for she was the first of the many thousands of washerwomen on the Seine, and the only one to enjoy a clean, if meagre, water-supply. I tried to photograph the scene, to capture something of the atmosphere of the place. But unfortunately, bemused by river-goddesses and lunch-time coq au vieux Bourgogne and Fleurie, I forgot to refocus my camera after taking a close-up of the nymph. I console myself with the thought that rarely has a place been less photogenic.

I strolled back up the stream. Four goats scampered away up the eastern side of the valley, among the oaks and ashes and sycamores. I found myself once more facing the grotto and the nymph and the pool. Sequana is not dead, I reflected. The cult lives on in its modern, Roman form. The whole floor of the pool glittered with the coins thrown in by the faithful pilgrims. Dutifully I added my franc.

3

I have a theory that the destruction of Sequana's temple was not only due to routine vandalism, 'because it was there'. I think it was provoked by the fact that she was a female, and the Germans have no taste for venerating women, whether they be queens, goddesses or saints. It was the Franks from the Rhine who introduced the Salic Law into Gaul; and it was the Burgundians, whether they themselves destroyed the shrine or not, who suppressed the cult of Sequana. At the other end of the history of independent Burgundy we find them instrumental in destroying another holy girl, Joan of Arc. So it must have been a source of satisfaction to them that when Sequana next appeared on the historical scene in AD 542, she had undergone a remarkable sex-change and had become a most masculine monk, Saint Seigne.

However, despite this, the Seine remains a feminine river, *la* Seine, like the Loire, and the Garonne; and unlike the Rhône, the Rhine and the Danube. I do not know for certain what determines the sex of rivers, but I expect that they take their sex from their titulary god or goddess. And it is no coincidence that the Rhône, the Rhine and the Danube all rise in Teutonic lands.

Saint Seigne is, unlike Sequana, a far from mythological character, even if one of the sources did burst out where his donkey happened to kneel down, in the great wood on the hill above Sequana's ruined temple. (The site was marked by an engraved stone, but it has been recently stolen, for some mysterious purpose.) The son of the Comte de Mesmont, he was given as much land as he could ride round in a day on his donkey. As usual in versions of this story, he managed an amazing mileage. He then settled down to converting all the people who lived in the woods from their ancient faith – and we can guess what that was. He was at pains to emphasize the more Christian aspects of waters and rivers. At the abbey founded by him at what is now Saint-Seine-l'Abbaye, there is a fresco of Saint Seigne in his black monk's robe presenting a traveller to the Infant Jesus who is in the middle of the river on Saint Christopher's back. Outside the abbey there is an eighteenth-century fountain, on the site of an older one, showing Christ and the woman of Samaria. Saint Seigne tried hard; it wasn't his fault that he was turned into a river-god.

He was also a great benefactor to his people. He started the practice whereby the villagers who lived round his abbey could cut and take their firewood free from his woods, and in particular from the wood above the sources of the Seine. He encouraged the people to clear the land and plant crops; indeed, he became a harvest saint and his day is the third Sunday in September. But the connection with the river persisted. There are reports, according to Marcel Bonnefoy, that in the eighteenth century the villagers of Saint-Seine-l'Abbaye would go in procession to the sources of the Seine six miles away and there sprinkle their priest with the holy river water.

Nowadays the abbey is at pains to disclaim any connection with the sources of the Seine. 'Très peu de rapport', I was told. The Saint's day is a simple harvest festival, the procession merely goes round the village. Saint-Seine-l'Abbaye no longer owns all the surrounding countryside. But it still owns the wood above the sources of the Seine; and the inhabitants still make the six-mile journey there to cut their free firewood.

4

I was staying at Saint-Seine-l'Abbaye and on the way back Jean-Paul, he of the red nose, stopped on the hill outside the village so that I might admire the view. It is a very pretty village, nestling in a steep fold of the hills, huddled round its abbey. The walls are generally of grey stone, with grey stone roofs, though these are now being replaced little by little by tiles. The general effect is reminiscent of a Cotswold village.

I returned to Saint-Seine in some trepidation. I had gone to the local garage some hours before and asked for a taxi to take me to the sources of the Seine. It appeared that there was none, but Jean-Paul, who worked there, suggested that we borrow Madame's car which happened to be in the garage. She herself would be in the hairdresser's for the next hour or two.

'But won't she mind?' I asked.

He shrugged.

'Anyway, who is Madame?' I asked.

He threw up his hands. 'Madame, oh ho ho! She is the wife of the Commandant.' He added cryptically, 'Many stripes on his arm.'

Now returning some hours later, I was expecting to find Madame, and probably the Commandant, and possibly all his armed forces, brooding furiously on the hijacking of the car.

Madame indeed was waiting, but she was charming and not in the least put out. Had I enjoyed the trip, what did I think of it? I explained the reasons for my interest in the Seine. In that case, she said, if I wanted to find out more about Saint Seigne, she would walk up to the abbey with me and introduce me to a lady who was the local expert and would tell me all there was to be known. I accepted her offer gratefully.

It was the first of hundreds of kindnesses I found wherever I went on my wanderings. If anyone, sore after an acrimonious encounter with a Paris taxi-driver or porter, begins to feel that the French have forgotten their traditional hospitality, I recommend a journey down the Seine. In the end, I came almost to take it for granted that at the very sight of me, everyone would rush to give me their time or lend me their car or boat.

Madame duly handed me over to an elderly grey-haired lady, who told me all about Saint Seigne and his traditions. I think she was a little surprised, as she had expected me to be more interested in the abbey and its history. Indeed, it is a fine church, early thirteenth century in the transition from Romanesque to Gothic. The abbey continued until the Revolution when the monks were driven out and the adjoining cloisters became a private house. Now it is a school for backward children.

I thanked her warmly and congratulated her on her knowledge. It was nothing, she told me. She had been born on the site and had lived there all her life. Her name, wonderfully, was Mademoiselle Lemoine – Miss Monk.

Saint-Seine-l'Abbaye has a quiet triangular square, with benches and lime trees and stacks of cut firewood from Sequana's wood. It also has a picturesque old inn, with a courtyard gurgling with water from the Samaritaine fountain at the abbey. Its restaurant has an excellent chef and there in due course I found coeur de filet Rossini and a soufflé au Grand Marnier. I also found the car-park full of cars with GB plates and the dining-room thick with English voices telling each other about other good meals they had eaten. After dinner I found an inebriated Scotsman who lectured the barmaid for two hours on the superiority of whisky, porridge for breakfast and British eating habits in general, until he passed out on the floor. Luckily for her, she spoke no English.

5

I continued my journey by bus. Bus is perhaps my favourite form of travel – cheap, quick, going from village to village, with fine opportunities for looking at the view and talking to the local population. Further, if a village is suddenly appealing, nothing is easier than to step off and catch the next one a couple of hours later. And this particular bus followed the Seine for most of its journey.

Catching the bus was an ice-breaking experience. Six of us were waiting for it when it arrived from Dijon, crowded to the doors. 'Je suis complet,' the driver shouted, 'je ne prends personne.' The gesture made, he then waited while we all forced ourselves on somehow. I found myself wedged between two enormous Burgundian women, the very antithesis, it seemed, of little Sequana. Between their great arms, I peered out at the view.

It was a very English landscape, a rolling countryside like the Yorkshire Wolds or the Cotswolds. There were scattered woods, on the hillsides, of oak, ash and sycamore. Nut trees grew at odd corners of fields, and there were even some hedges. There were none of the familiar symbols of France, not an olive tree, not a vine, hardly a poplar. We passed through little stone villages, and I felt as if I were in Gloucestershire. The only jarring features were the splashes of brilliant yellow, the mustard fields – for the Côte d'Or is, amongst other things, mustard country.

We were on a plateau. The Seine, la petite Seine as it is officially called, was still in its steep valley on our left. We crossed it at Courceau, a muddy trickle squelching through a farm. It then made a substantial loop on our right, collected a couple of tributaries, the Revinson and the Coquille, and came back to us. At Saint-Marc it was a definite river, a yard or more wide, clear, lined with trees. There I first became aware of one of the Seine's greatest features, its fishermen. Yes, I was told, Saint-Marc was a good place for fishing, la petite Seine was full of trout.

As the Seine widened, so did the valley. It was no longer a narrow cleft but a broad trough a mile or more wide. The plateau was still harvest stubble or mustard, the sides of the valley wooded like green curtains, the floor of the valley pasturage, water-meadows, full of Châtillon cows, brown like Jerseys, and like Jerseys providers of the cream so essential to Burgundian cooking. Among the meadows the Seine wriggled about like vermicelli; one of the characteristics of the Seine is that at no stage from the source to the sea does it feel the need to follow a straight course. Every few hundred yards was a water-mill, grinding corn or mustard or cutting wood. The Seine may be a meandering leisurely river, but it does a lot of work on its way.

We passed through a string of pleasant villages, Saint-Marc, Aisey, Nod, Chamesson, Buncey. Aisey is probably the prettiest, and it has an inn which prides itself on its cooking. Then, abruptly it seemed, the bus stopped and we were being squeezed out like toothpaste into the hard modern square of Châtillon-sur-Seine.

6

What is the first reaction of a travel-writer to a new town? What is the first thing he does? Each one has his individual preference. Dame Rose Macaulay liked to go to the nearest ruins to check their ivy-covering. Ian Fleming usually went to the police station to find out about the local crime. Other, living writers seem to head for the nearest Michelin-starred restaurant. Myself, I seem to go first to the nearest café for wine and cheese.

They go well together, especially if you have missed lunch. Wine and cheese parties, indeed, are a leit-motif of London in the sixties. The very words recall Chelsea parties, poetry readings, hard shiny Cheddar and Portuguese claret. But in the Café Europe in Châtillon I wasn't bothered by such associations. Everything was local here, the wine Passetoutgrain and the cheese Epoisses.

Burgundian wine and cooking are justly famous all over the world. Burgundian cheese is, equally justly, unknown outside Burgundy. A few days earlier in Dijon, I had opened my exploration of that city with a private wine and cheese party in a café. Chaource, I was assured by everyone sitting nearby, was the finest of Burgundian cheeses, indeed possibly the finest of all cheeses. I had been sadly disappointed in Chaource. I like a soft cheese with un bon goût and this was dry, chalky and tasteless.

Everyone round me had been amazed. But it was a delicious cheese, they explained, with an unusually high percentage of fat matter. I mentioned some of my favourite strong cheeses, Pont l'Evêque, Livarot, Munster. They all grimaced with disgust. They would never eat such cheeses, they declared, I would never find those in Burgundy, who could possibly want to buy them? Soumaintrain was the strongest of local cheeses, it was like a Langres, I would assuredly find that to my taste. But alas that café in Dijon did not have it; indeed, the proprietor did not seem to have heard of it.

I was going through pretty much the same scene now in

Châtillon. The patron was amazed that I did not care for Chaource. How was that possible, he asked. But anyway there were other cheeses that I would certainly like. Here was Epoisses, would I try that? It was altogether different from Chaource, very fine, with an unusually high percentage of fat matter and un très bon goût.

Alas, I found Epoisses indistinguishable from Chaource. Had he any Soumaintrain? The patron shook his head in bewilderment. No, he did not know that name. But would I not help myself to some more Epoisses? Assuredly I would like it now.

I consoled myself, quite easily, with the wine, which was smooth and light. Then, fortified but not comatose, I set out to see the treasure of Vix.

7

The great vase of Vix stands by itself in the Châtillon museum. The first sight of it makes you gasp; it is so beautiful, and so big. It stands about five foot six high (1 metre 64 cm to be exact), and on its pedestal that means that you cannot see the inside. It is almost as wide as it is high, but such are its proportions, its natural grace, that it has none of the feeling of squatness, of pot-belly that you expect in a vessel as broad as it is tall. It is made of bronze, cast in one piece, beaten out cold and polished. In any age it would have been a masterpiece of metallurgy, but in the sixth century BC it was an amazing feat.

Round the neck of the vase, attached by tiny rivets, a military frieze marches endlessly round and round, soldier, horses, charioteer, soldier, horses, charioteer, round and round the walls of Troy for ever. The two handles (purely decorative, for you could never hope to lift the vase by them empty, much less full) are on a different artistic scale, though in shape and in proportion they are integral to the general form. From the frieze to the handles you move from history to myth, from factual detail of military equipment to fearful legend. The curling handles are joined to the vase by two gorgons, grimacing, their tongues out, their faces grinning and contemptuous, hooked on by their arms, their legs turning at the knees into serpents. This is a long way from Homer, even from the legendary Perseus. These are spirits from much farther east, visitors, so it seemed to me, from the Indian mythology.

From the front you can hardly see them. You are back in the world of Greek grace and proportion, of European plenty, of great thirsts and gargantuan appetites. The vase holds, the guardian told me, eleven hundred litres of wine. He also told me, I fear incorrectly, that they found traces of wine in the earth at the bottom. Still, there is no doubt that it was intended for wine. Herodotus writes that the Spartans made a large bronze vase with a frieze of figures and a capacity of three hundred amphorae of wine, as a grovelling present for King Croesus; and it is possible, just possible, that this vase found its way to Vix. Certainly Croesus never got it. Out of some typically Mediterranean double-dealing, the vase came into the possession of the Samians.

Dash down yon cup of Samian wine! But you couldn't dash this cup down, even empty. How did they move it? How did they fill it and, even harder, empty it? It must have all been done on the same spot and, when it was half empty, they must have had to stand on ladders scooping it out. I stood before it, thinking about eleven hundred litres of wine, local wine. It is thought that the Greeks originally introduced the vine to France; the same vines on the same soil under the same sky. Or were the vines, the climate, the earth, the wine quite different? I hope not. I like to think of that great vase full of eleven hundred litres of Passetoutgrain, or Fleurie, or Brouilly, or Chambertin, the biggest carafe in the world, the grandest cornucopia, the epitome, a thousand years before the coming of the Burgundians, of Burgundy.

Vix is a small village some three miles north of Châtillon at the foot of a wooded hill called Mont Lassois. There was found in January 1953 the burial mound of a princess. She had been buried there towards the end of the sixth century BC, lying on her ornamental carriage, from which the wheels had been removed, surrounded by her treasures: a gold diadem, bronzes, ornaments, jewellery, Etruscan vases, Athenian cups, and, of course, the great vase. A great treasure in any age; and at a time when metal was scarce and distances were long, astounding.

It is too easily assumed, no doubt after a surfeit of Caesar's *Gallic War*, that the Romans were the first civilized people encountered by the barbaric tribes of Gaul. The tribes were far from barbaric, and the Greeks had been there, trading and settling, five or six centuries before the Romans. And even they, it is now thought, may have been following in the footsteps of the Minoans and the Mycenaeans.

Mont Lassois had been a trading centre from even earlier. There are traces of occupation ever since Neolithic man. But it gained its chief importance about the end of the iron age, during the sixth century BC. On the old overland tin-route to Britain and surrounded by rich iron-age tycoons able to buy gold diadems or great vases from Greece, it commanded the Seine valley at the point where the merchandise was transhipped. Coming from the Mediterranean, from Marseilles up the Rhône and the Saone, across land to the Seine, it turned Mont Lassois for those hundred years into the great entrepôt centre, the Hong Kong of ancient Gaul. It is certain that the vase was made in pre-classical Greece about 580 BC either in Sparta or Corinth, according to whether you follow the French or German theory. But it is a long journey, by sea, river and land, and the mind boggles at the thought of transporting it intact on that complicated journey. What organisers those Greek traders must have been, and how rich the moguls of Mont Lassois! And how pious to bury it in the cemetery at Vix only sixty or seventy years later!

Who was she, this princess who received this honour? We only know that she was quite young, between thirty and thirty-five, and that she deserved having so much treasure from such distant lands buried beside her. I hope that the great vase was full of wine at the start of her funeral and empty at the end. It must have been a magnificent wake, worthy of one who, it seemed to me that afternoon in front of the vase, could only have been another incarnation of Sequana.

8

Châtillon, lying on the routes from Paris to the Rhône valley and Geneva, has been a centre of much military activity. Napoleon rejected the allied surrender terms there in 1814; Garibaldi tried and failed to relieve it when it was occupied by the invading Germans in 1870; Joffre had his headquarters there during the battle of the Marne; Leclerc and de Lattre de Tassigny, the one from Normandy, the other from the Mediterranean, met there in August 1940. None of these events left any visible traces on the town, except some street names and monuments.

But an air-raid by the Italians in 1940 did a great deal of damage, burning down the whole town centre, the area round what is now the Place de la Résistance. It has all now been rebuilt in modern style, stone-faced, homogeneous without being monotonous, and it will look quite well when it has weathered in. But the spare newness of this part has given the general idea that Châtillon is a place of little interest, a town to leave quickly once you have seen the Vix treasure.

I do not agree. The museum building itself, the Maison Philandrier, is a graceful Renaissance building with an unexpected Italian tower. And the old town huddled between the Seine and the escarpment is untouched and picturesque.

So it seemed to me as I wandered along a narrow street, my mind so full of the great vase that I did not see a wedding procession coming towards me till it was almost upon me. The bride and bridegroom, leading, were keeping a fairly steady course, but the procession behind had taken an ample amount of wine, if not the full eleven hundred litres. They were cannoning off the walls of that little street like billiard-balls. I waved to the bride and ducked out of the way, under an arch about five feet high, into the rue des Evolots.

It was deserted but a small girl came out of a doorway and asked if she could help me. I explained that I was merely admiring the pretty street. She gazed at me dumbfounded as I went on up the street, climbing to the top of the escarpment. At the top there is a dilapidated eleventh-century church, Saint Vorlès, commanding the town and a wide panorama of the Seine valley.

The Seine splits into two rather meagre streams at Châtillon, and opposite the town football ground the right branch receives the most spectacular tributary in the whole length of the Seine, the Douix. It pours out from under the escarpment, which at this point is a sheer limestone cliff, hanging with ivy and box, and crowned with trees. It emerges in a rush, a fully fledged river, bubbling, sparkling, with green weeds waving glassily. Past boulders, under a small bridge, past a promenade of huge chestnuts, past mothers pushing prams, it plunges into the Seine. One hundred yards of life and it is all over. The Douix has a source Sequana would have envied, and at the point of confluence, it is a bigger river than the Seine. But the Seine is a holy river, and the Seine accepts it and absorbs it, just as it had earlier absorbed the Revinson and the Coquille, and as it would later accept the Aube, the Yonne, the Loing, the Marne, the Oise.

It was a peaceful place. I sat on a bench from where I could see the whole length of the Douix. High above me were the chestnuts, gold in the evening sunlight. Birds shrilled and flapped, passers-by greeted me, the river gurgled. After the treasure of Vix, the Douix is the second attraction of the town.

Châtillon has a third attraction, a Michelin-starred restaurant. After my experiences at Saint-Seine I kept well clear. Instead I spent the evening in a big brasserie, surrounded by large friendly Burgundians eating snails, and poulet à la crême, and Chaource.

9

From Châtillon I went north, by the road to Troyes, past Vix, past Mont Lassois. It was still the same English valley, wooded hillsides, pastures at the valley bottom, sleepy cows, stony villages. A sunny Sunday morning in the Cotswolds with the trees starting to turn, and the only suggestions of France were the occasional house painted green, or the shutters mauve. Beside me on my left was the little Seine, twisting and turning, encased in trees, like an endless green and coppery worm. Only at the mills could you catch the flash of water.

But there were mills everywhere – sawmills, flour mills, mustard mills. Most of the mustard of France must come from hereabouts, I reflected. Burgundian mustard, Dijon mustard, the mustard you find with every bifteck and entrecôte, made with wine, not vinegar, and tasting very like ordinary English mustard. What has happened, I wondered, to that brown vinegary paste called French mustard? Is it now only found in Surrey?

At Gommeville something happens quite suddenly to the landscape. The valley widens into undulating countryside, there is plough beside the river, and the hillsides are sometimes bare and stony with the gleam of chalk. I asked my neighbour, a large grey friendly woman in her best Sunday suit. Yes, indeed it was chalk, she said. We had now left the Côte d'Or and were in Aube, we were leaving Burgundy and were entering Champagne.

In Gyé-sur-Seine there were decorative vines on the fronts of some of the houses. 'Look!' said my neighbour. On the hillside above us was a small stony vineyard. They were the first and only vines I saw on the whole journey. Beside the road was a big poster advertising champagne; indeed, there was a champagne feel in the air, though my neighbour was undoubtedly Burgundian.

Was there lots of cheap champagne locally, I asked her. Could anyone make his own private supply?

'Oh no,' she said. 'It is all controlled, you have to have permission to plant vines, any vines.'

She explained the system to me, a sort of co-operative arrangement, for making and selling champagne. At Neuville the champagne factory was on the right of the road, the selling agency on the left. It seemed a convenient plan.

'Yes, it is cheaper than in Paris,' she said. 'But still only for special occasions.'

'What do you do for every day? Is there a local red wine?'

She grimaced. 'It is very sharp. You see, it is grown on poor soil, or on slopes without enough sun. You must never grow grapes for red wine near champagne grapes in case they cross-breed.'

She left me with a friendly farewell at Polisot. Her place was taken by another large Burgundian, a man. The bus seats seem so narrow in this part of France. I asked him about the local wines, and he took up the conversation where his predecessor had left it. He fitted in to the dialogue like a duplicate key.

No, he certainly did not recommend me the local red wine, it was very rough.

I said, 'But in Champagne they are connoisseurs of wine. Why do they put up with it?' He laughed.

I told him that I drank vin ordinaire regularly in Paris, and elsewhere. But the only unswallowable wine I had found was in the bus station in Dijon. And there I was surrounded by Burgundians, all presumably connoisseurs of red wine, drinking the terrible stuff without alarm.

My friend said, 'If they cannot afford Beaune, they must drink what they can'.

'But why don't they demand something better? Why don't they protest?'

He laughed again. The suggestion of protest often causes laughter in France.

'Listen,' he said. 'You must never drink vin ordinaire in regions of France where there are great wines, Champagne, Burgundy, Bordeaux. All the best soil is given to the great wines. The little that is left over is hardly suitable for vines at all. Vin ordinaire may be all right in Paris, in the Dordogne or Auvergne. But never in Champagne or Burgundy.'

I was surprised by his implication that vin ordinaire is local wine. I had always assumed that it came from any and everywhere, a mish-mash of the poorer French wines, Spanish, Algerian, Australian, blended in huge tanks by faceless labelless wholesalers, tested for alcohol and acidity, and marketed in bulk. It is surprising how drinkable it usually is.

10

I was so captivated by the sight of Bar-sur-Seine that I said a brief farewell to my new friend, grabbed my case and jumped off the bus. Bar is indeed delightful with its picturesque streets, old houses, several of them half timbered. Bar was once the frontier village of the Duchy of Burgundy (though the name implies that there was at least an outpost at Bourguignons, a mile or two further on), fortified and fought over. But the only relic of the fortifications is a clock tower standing improbably alone among the thick trees on the hill above the village, and Bar is a quiet sleepy place. A seventeenth-century gateway has made the main street impassable to modern traffic and a by-pass has been built, channelling away the noise.

I crossed the by-pass and strolled down to the Seine a few hundred yards away. It was an unexpected sight. Since I had last seen it, during the time I had been talking about wine, it had grown, abruptly and unseen, from a stream a yard or two wide to a brimming river fifty-seven paces wide – I paced it on the bridge. I had the same unnerving feeling I remember from playing Grandmother's Steps as a child; you turned away your head for only an instant and someone the far side of the lawn was breathing down your neck.

I suppose it was the result of all the mills and dams making the river wider and shallower, though it had in fact received three small tributaries since the Douix. The river is dammed again at Bar, and a power-station has been installed inside the old flour mill built out over the river. The Seine turns the turbines in a quiet hum of industrial activity, the first of its major projects.

I stood on the bridge watching the rural scene. The bank was lined with Sunday fishermen, both above and below the mill. The banks are grassy, wild, for the village turns its back on the river and faces introspectively into its own past. Below me the river was glassy, green, still fairly clear, flowing very slowly towards

Troyes. For this was a place or a day when the Seine definitely, if reluctantly, flowed downstream.

The church of Bar is a pleasant mixture of Gothic and Renaissance art. I waited by the imposing Renaissance portal while a large congregation filed out after mass. After a while I gave up and went round to the side door. The service was over but the organ was still playing, children and nuns were fluttering about. The inside is a tall Gothic church and the grisaille windows would give much pleasure to those who admire grisaille windows. I fear I am not among them. To me stained glass is essentially a jewelled art, a subtle pattern of reds and blues glowing in the darkness of an ambulatory. Elaborate sepia drawings in full perspective, realistic pictures of saints and martyrdoms carefully showing the folds of the robes or the muscles of the upper arm are doubtless a logical extension of Renaissance draughtmanship. They leave me yearning for the colours of Chartres.

I concentrated instead on the fine classical balconies. In the narthex a nun was selling booklets to a line of children. Keen not to miss anything, I queued up and bought one too. The children seemed unsurprised and the nun gave me a sweet smile as if she were giving me the Thoughts of Sainte-Therèse of Lisieux. In fact, it seemed to be a magazine about the various doings of pop-idols, and the cover was a colour photograph of Claude François, the singer. It was an unexpected purchase to make in a church.

I went out, through the little square, through an old coach-yard into the street, the rue Victor Hugo. How monotonous are the names of French streets! Every English or American town does not find it necessary to have a Charles Dickens Square or a Mark Twain Street. But there cannot be a town or village in France without its rue Victor Hugo or its Place Maréchal Foch, irrespective of whether those heroes ever came near the place or not. And the heroes are so few, drawn from such a very short list. Always the same three writers, Hugo, Zola, Voltaire (never Balzac, Stendhal or Proust); always the same three Marshals, Foch, Joffre, Leclerc (never Turenne, Masséna or Ney); always the same three statesmen, Thiers, Clemenceau, de Gaulle (never Colbert,

Mirabeau or Talleyrand). Never, except on their own stamping-grounds, a painter, a composer, a king, an emperor or a saint.

I noticed that the village fromagerie was open, and I went in. 'Do you have Soumaintrain?' I asked.

Madame shook her head in puzzlement. The other customers all said, 'Comment?'

'Soumaintrain,' I said. 'It is a local cheese. Soumaintrain. Soumaintrain, Soumain-train.' I tried various pronunciations in case the failure might be in communication rather than in cheese supply.

A man in a black hat said at last that he knew the name but assuredly it was not a cheese.

'Without doubt it is a cheese from this region,' I said firmly. 'It is recommended specially by Michelin. It is strong like a Munster.'

This thought seemed to distress everyone. Madame said, 'I do not know that name. But I have many other cheeses from this region, Chaource, Epoisses, Pavillon, Gout d'Or, Saint-Florentin, Hervy. Without doubt you would find all of them delicious. They contain an exceptionally high percentage of fat matter. Voilà!'

I said regretfully that no, it had to be Soumaintrain and I apologized for taking up her time. Everyone looked at me strangely.

Outside in the street I reflected that it did not seem to be a good day for a wine and cheese party. Besides I was hungry. I went to the village inn and was installed at a table looking out at the little square glowing in the sunlight. Before me was a red tablecloth, above me was a stuffed boar's head. There, with pâté de sanglier, jambon à la crême, coq au vin and Chaource, I ate a suitable farewell to Burgundy.

11

Troyes! The very word is like a fanfare of trumpets at a tournament. Troyes, the ancient capital, the pride of Champagne, the city of the great fairs and the great feasts, of joustings and knightings, of barons in silken hose and ladies in wimples, of poets and troubadours, of merchants bargaining and Crusaders vowing and esquires wenching and drinking, and the flutter of banners over everything. You arrive, expecting the place to look like a scene from the Book of Hours.

Incredibly, it still almost does, at least in the old town. Not, of course, the shining castles on the hill, but the huddle of medieval houses crowded together inside the old walls. The streets are narrow and tortuous and have evocative names – the rue du Marché au Pain, rue du Marché aux Noix, rue des Changes. The houses are old and rickety, half-timbered, the upper storey hanging out over the street; in the rue des Chats the roofs actually meet overhead. The grander houses are often embellished with lantern windows or turrets, and at the end of every street is a stone church tower rising over the picturesque maze; for Troyes is a town of many churches. From my bedroom window I looked out at a film-set of steep tiled roofs and dark alleys and soaring grey buttresses. A few feet away the clock of Sainte-Madeleine played the first three notes of Three Blind Mice all through the day.

Troyes has a long history. Before the Germans invented the Schlieffen plan, the right hook through Belgium, the traditional route for the invaders was through Champagne, and Troyes started by being simply a fortress on the Seine. Attila, though he burnt Rheims and the surrounding countryside, spared Troyes because of the devotion of the Bishop, Saint Loup, who offered himself as a hostage. As the capital of the Counts of Champagne, the city prospered and grew. It became a centre of feudal society and religion – Count Henri I alone built thirteen churches. A centre too of literature and the arts; it was Marie, the wife of Henri I, who commanded the local poet Chrétien de Troyes to write his romances of the court of King Arthur – the start, it may be argued, of the French novel if not of French literature, and the inspiration of Malory and Tennyson and much else. It was Marie's grandson, Thibaut the Fourth, another poet, who founded the great fairs to which merchants from all over Europe and even Asia came. Pope Urban IV was born there; Henry V of England signed in 1420 the notorious Treaty of Troyes, which illegitimized the Dauphin and proclaimed Henry Regent and his future son King of France. It was in the church of Saint-Jean, a narrow Gothic building like two churches pushed end to end, that he married Katharine of France and sealed the Treaty. Joan of Arc, nine years later, drove out the English without much difficulty, riding in at the head of her troops. In the following century the Guises were there, and the city was involved in the Wars of Religion. Indeed, from Roman times till the sixteenth century the story of Troyes is the story of France.

And at that point the story of Troyes ceases. The reasons for its decline are gradual and several. Indeed, they start as far back as 1284 when Philippe le Bel of France married Jeanne of Champagne and joined the two countries together. The stigma of the English occupation, the persecution of the Huguenots, of which there were a great number in Troyes, the ending of the international fairs, the revocation of the Edict of Nantes, all played their part. Troyes was left behind, a small provincial town beside the unnavigable Seine, full of old houses and old churches, thinking only of hosiery and pork.

Now even the pork has gone. In the abattoirs beside the Seine under the great plane trees, they now slaughter beef. The pork has to be imported from elsewhere.

The taxi driver, who brought me from the bus station, wanted to take me to a hotel in a quiet street in a suburb, and was amazed when I insisted on one in the old town. 'But you will not like it there,' he said. 'It is dirty.'

I said how pretty it was, but he did not follow me.

'They are pulling it down where they can, but they often cannot get the tenants out.'

In surprise I found that this was the standard view. When I remarked to the patronne of a café about the charm of the old streets, she said apologetically:

'We are trying to get the tenants out, but it is difficult. They seem to like being there and they often have no water or plumbing. But when we can get them out, we lock the house and put up a demolition order. Then we wait for it to fall down. We shall rebuild it all in the end.'

In parts they are hastening the process of decay. A woman shopping at a greengrocer's near the rue du Gros Raisin told me with satisfaction that the whole area round there and the rue de l'Eau Benite was to be pulled down and turned into a municipal garden. Sadly, I could imagine the end-product only too clearly.

A few houses in fact have been restored as showpieces, usually those with a prominent turret or window. But elsewhere the erosion of time is working only too well, with crumbling plaster, broken laths and often a hole in the wall to show the dereliction inside. It would, I reflected, thinking of Stratford-on-Avon or York, be very different if Troyes were in England. There would be grants for restoration, the quarter would be a mass of tea-shops and book-shops and antique-shops and copper bedwarmers, and everyone would be saying that it was spoilt and commercialized. It must, it seemed to me, be one extreme or the other.

For Troyes is indifferent to its history, to the treasure in its midst. You do not see posters advertising the town on railway stations or tourist offices. There are no son et lumière, no guides, no floodlighting, no coach tours, no souvenir shops. There are few hotels and restaurants and it is difficult even to buy a postcard.

'Why do you not publish a brochure about the town?' I asked the patronne of Au Petit Vatel.

She shrugged. 'But who would pay for that? We should have to.'

So they are quietly letting old Troyes fall down, and rebuilding it piecemeal where they can – including a horrid little concrete cube in the middle of the rue des Chats. Looking at the town's modern architecture, the new post office, the Resistance Memorial ('pas mal' said my taxi driver, and I hope he was referring to the number of names on it, and not to its design) I can see no very beautiful future for Troyes.

Part of the difficulty is that the French find it very hard to admire any architecture before the Renaissance, other than cathedrals. In particular they are antipathetic to the sort of picturesque corners which so delight the British and the Americans. They like their buildings to be splendid and spacious, and it is no coincidence that the one secular building which I saw being carefully scrubbed and restored was the town hall, partly no doubt because it was the town hall and partly because it has a Renaissance façade.

A further difficulty is that Troyes is not a proud name in French history. The Treaty is a matter for shame still; Joan of Arc did her greatest deeds elsewhere; neither the Sun King nor the Emperor ever came near the place. And the final difficulty, I suggest, is cash. Troyes is no longer particularly prosperous and it has, thanks to Henri I, an inordinate number of old churches to keep up. To restore and modernize a few thousand old houses as well would be a daunting task for the local ratepayers. But it seemed to me that an injection of financial help might well stimulate local pride. When the Blessed Marguerite Bourgeoys went to Canada, Paul de Chomedey wrote, in 1653, of 'Champagne which seems to wish to give to this place (Montreal) more than all the other provinces put together'. Troyes did a great deal for Montreal in the seventeenth century. Perhaps that great and rich city might now repay a little of its debt.

12

I lingered in Troyes, murmuring to myself the immortal words, 'Emily, this is a four day city'. I wandered through the narrow streets in a medieval dream. I looked at some of the remarkable churches – Saint-Pantaleon, a hive of hammering workmen; Saint-Jean with its fine vaulting; Sainte-Madeleine with its splendid balcony, a stone riot of arches and foliage and figures; Saint-Nizier with its coloured patterned roof; and, the finest of all, Saint-Urbain.

Pope Urban IV started the church to glorify his birthplace, a humble shoemaker's shop. It also involved pulling down a nunnery, and the nuns protested, driving out the workmen, the abbess herself slapping the bishop. For this she and all her nuns were excommunicated. But despite this unhappy start, the church is a wonder of harmony and Gothic design, a soaring creation ot pinnacles and flying buttresses. The choir rises in one single springing arch, and the windows are enormous. Indeed, the walls are really curtains of glass, and the church is reminiscent, and not

unworthy, of the Sainte-Chapelle itself. But unfortunately large
windows need great designers and though Troyes is proud of its
stained glass and was from the fourteenth century to the seventeenth a centre of that art, it seemed to me that great craftsmanship
and meticulousness and attention were not always matched by
equal feats of imagination.

For great stained glass you have to go to the cathedral. Here,
too, much of the glass seems to me uninspired. Delicate, detailed
so that they are really oil-paintings on glass, the effect is lost at a
distance in a big building. But the difference between the ped-
estrian and the inspired is enormous, and the best windows are
magnificent. In the choir and the ambulatory they glow with a
splendour which recalls the glory that is Chartres.

The cathedral façade, like so many others in France, is asymmetrical. There is one strong stone tower on the north side and it
was there during the religious wars of the sixteenth century that
the Catholic governor, Claude de Guise, a scion of the famous
family, took refuge during a siege by the royalist army. One
should not perhaps blame him too much for his lack of valour, for
he was only eleven years old. However, the Catholics fell back
and the Protestant troops entered the city. But, while still in the
outskirts, they were tempted by the famous andouillettes, the
speciality of the town. They ate so many that they became comatose and the Catholic League forces, rallying under a more experi-
enced commander, counter-attacked successfully, killing the
torpid guzzlers in hundreds.

A cautionary tale, I felt, for gastronomes. But what were these
andouillettes, which had caused such havoc to the royalist army?
In search of more detailed information, I went into an épicerie
near the cathedral and asked the owner. Yes indeed he had andouillettes, the andouillettes of Troyes were delicious and famous.
They were like sausages, open-ended, made of pigs' intestines,
salted, peppered, seasoned, rolled in flour. He made his own,
would I not like to take some away and try them, they were no
trouble to cook. I thanked him but explained that I had at the
moment no place to do any cooking.

However, I went immediately to the nearest restaurant and

ordered one. Of course, said madame, everyone came to Troyes to eat andouillettes. It tasted almost exactly as I expected it to, by no means unpleasant, though I did not feel tempted to gorge myself into a stupor on them. Perhaps tastes were different in the sixteenth century. But if the andouillettes were really so irresistible, why were the Catholic League troops not equally stuffed and sleepy? Or were they sick of the things, were andouillettes only for visitors, tourists? Or was it a religious difference, did the attack take place on a Friday? And what was that great soldier Henry of Navarre doing to allow his troops to become so easily demoralized?

A word from the next table jerked me out of these musings. Soumaintrain. At last, Soumaintrain. A thin, sad young man was studying the cheeseboard. It was not strong, was it, he asked anxiously. Sadly I heard the waitress reassure him. But no, it was not strong at all.

When I came to taste it in my turn, I found she was all too right. Soumaintrain too tasted exactly as I expected, chalky and mild just like all the others. It was a disappointing lunch and I consoled myself with the thought that the Brie country lay just ahead.

Andouillettes apart, it seemed to me that the population of Troyes was chiefly partial to sea-food, surprising when I remembered how far away the sea still was. On all sides there seemed to be stalls of oysters, mussels, sea-urchins, prawns, soles, plaice, cod. After dining agreeably on oysters and haddock à l'anglaise, I would stroll to one of the cafés on the Place Maréchal Foch where the youth of Troyes congregated. They would sit about, drinking coffee, playing the pin-tables, fiddling with their lighters, buzzing off into the night on scooters. They were young, attractive, bored, many of them negroes, all to a man or a girl dressed for the ski-slopes, though it was a mild autumn night. They were the future rulers of Troyes, the future hosiery workers, and whatever their carefully concealed interests might be, it seemed unlikely that they would include the preservation of the old quarter. So if you want to see one of the last medieval cities of Europe, go soon. Gravity is not on your side.

13

A few miles to the east of Troyes, upstream, is one of the new projects for the Seine. It is a new artificial lake, with two canals for the entry and exit of water. The idea is to fill the lake during the winter and spring when the level of the Seine is high, and release it during the summer and autumn when the Seine is low and the proportion of noxious effluents unpleasantly large.

It seems a good idea and I have no doubt that the engineers have calculated the water levels with care. But I would be surprised if the scheme makes a great difference to the river. The Seine at Troyes is still a small river, too small for more than the odd rowing boat. The great tributaries still lie ahead, and I would have guessed that any height difference at Troyes would only have a marginal effect on the river in Paris. But the plan will provide a fine new amenity for Troyes, a brand new lake about the size of Annecy (though without the mountains), and it should provide a playground for fishermen, yachtsmen and birdwatchers. Development is inevitable, and I hope that the authorities will landscape the building into villages and not let it grow like a crust of cement round the water.

Troyes lies in flat country, for the hills are back in Burgundy. The tallest things you see, once you are out of the drab suburbs, are the poplars. For this is poplar country, and they are everywhere. Even, regular like guardsmen, in long straight lines, beside straight roads, straight tracks, straight canals, failing all else, beside nothing – and never beside the Seine which is never straight – they dominate the flat open landscape. Occasionally wild, sometimes planted for shade on a road or path (the avenue at Saint-Mesmin is especially fine), they are usually planted as a timber crop, by cuttings to prevent cross-pollination. They are carefully tended and harvested, as they are a valuable crop, used for houses, packing-cases, plywood, fruit or cheese boxes. With their height, clean shapes and unnatural regularity, they are the chief feature of that

bare ruled geometric countryside, across which the wooded Seine
moves so unexpectedly like an endless green squiggle.

The villages are less attractive than those in Burgundy, though I
always enjoy orchards, tiled roofs, piles of logs. But the outside of
every house has been refaced with roughcast cement, occasionally
embellished with dreadful fancy brickwork, and the result is
monotonous and displeasing. Even the big old church at Mazières-
la-grande-paroisse has been hideously restored with cement,
though the slated walls of the tower are eye-catching.

The people are different too, slimmer, less jovial, less smiling.
And though this made the buses more comfortable, the seats
wider, it seemed to me that something else besides bulk had gone.

Coming into Romilly, I brightened momentarily at the sight of
a placard BRIE-CHAMPAGNE. This, it seemed to me, might be the
finest wine and cheese party of them all. But a second glance
showed me that it was only an estate agent advertising houses in
those two districts. We passed a fair. Was this a Champagne fair, I
asked eagerly. I had visions of local buyers expertly tasting, of an
evening of great jollification.

Alas, no, said my neighbour sadly. It used to be, but now it was
just a roundabout and a few sideshows.

Romilly is an ugly little town, notable only for its flour mills
and its communism. Tactfully, the authorities have given the flour
contract for Red China to the local mills, and this seemed to give
much pleasure. Even the Mayor of Romilly is, reputedly, a
communist.

I changed buses in the square in front of the station. As I had
twenty minutes to spare, I went into the café. There was a notice
above the bar – 'Vivez joyeux, buvez la champagne – 1Fr 50 la
flute'. It was a concession to fairtime, and as my contribution to the
general jollity, I ordered a flute – a glass like a small inverted cone.

My neighbour, a young porter from the station, eyed me
doubtfully. Was I English, German? I said English.

Was I a communist?

I said no.

But why not? Why were there so few communists in England?
In France they were a large well-organized party.

I said cautiously that perhaps many possible communists in England were put off by the fact that the communist countries seemed to be simply imperialists like all the rest.

He shook his head sadly. 'Il faut changer tout ça,' he said.

I eyed the door, fearing I was about to be given a long lecture, but he said no more. Perhaps he had been inadequately briefed. Anyway, I finished my flute in silence. When I saw my bus arrive, I nodded at him and went out to join the bus queue.

It was one of those buses where you pay the driver and put your suitcase under the seat. Behind me was an old woman in black, who dropped some of her change as she paid the driver. We heard the rattle of the coins and someone scooped them up for her. She counted them carefully and apparently a fifty-centime piece was missing.

She had dropped a fifty-centime piece, she told us. Could we see it?

We all looked for it, but without result. Would we please all look again, she asked us. Assuredly it was here somewhere, she had heard it fall. Obediently we stood on our heads, poking around our luggage and our feet, but again without result.

Someone suggested that perhaps it had rolled out of the bus door on to the ground. Or perhaps she had never dropped it, perhaps it was still in her bag.

The woman would not hear of this. Certainly it was in the bus, on the floor. She had heard it roll away. Would we all please lift our luggage on to our seats, so that we could see the floor better.

Dutifully I hauled out my suitcase and stood on my head again. So did everybody else. But again it was with no success. We put back our luggage, sat down and looked out at the view. I hoped the bus would start soon. The woman stood by the driver surveying us. She was not beaten yet.

Down she went on her hands and knees, on the far from clean floor, nosing, snuffling round our feet and luggage like a large black shiny dog. Her granddaughter, a girl of fourteen or so, raised her eyes to the roof. 'All this for fifty centimes!' she groaned. She was told sharply to shut up and help with the search.

Grunting, fumbling, the woman worked her way to the back.

The bus filled up behind her, over her, round her. Finally she stood up.

She had still not found her fifty centimes, she informed us. So she must ask us all to take our luggage right out of the bus so that she could look under our seats better.

Meekly, amazingly, people began to obey. Something had to be done urgently. Surreptitiously I searched in my pocket for a fifty-centime piece, bent down, and exclaimed, 'Voilà!'

The woman gazed suspiciously at the coin. Where had I found it? I pointed at my feet. Had I not looked there then? All the world was helping her look for her coin and all the time it was under my feet. She addressed all the world. Look at her clothes! Dirty. Look at her hands, her stockings! All dirty! And all the time her fifty centimes had been under my feet.

All the world glowered at me; only the granddaughter grinned. I sympathized with her anger, it must have been tremendously irritating. But, all the same, I was quite glad that it was only a ten-minute drive to my destination, Marcilly.

14

I felt hungry and went into the first buvette in Marcilly, and there the following dialogue took place:

Could I please have some bread and cheese? – Non.

What, no cheese? – Non.

Not even Camembert? – Non.

Couldn't I even have a sandwich? – Non. Perhaps a sandwich.

What sort of sandwich? – Cheese.

What sort of cheese? – Camembert.

Good. And could I have a half bottle of Côte du Rhone? – Non.

And later I would like to go for a row on the Seine. Was there anyone in Marcilly who would lend me a boat? – Non.

In due course they brought me a plate of bread and Camembert (not a sandwich), and my wine, and told me that perhaps the wife of the Mayor of Marcilly might lend me her boat if I asked her.

Two or three hundred yards upstream of the village is the point where the Seine meets the Aube. The Aube is much the larger river, but it is not holy and so the Seine swallows it up. The two rivers are in great contrast: the Seine winding along in its green tunnel, and the Aube open with towpaths and boats and houses. And the Aube, though swallowed by the Seine, changes the Seine. From Marcilly onwards the Seine too is open, with towpaths and boats under a great sky. Marcilly is the highest point on the Seine which the barges can reach; and the first point where the scenic possibilities of the river are appreciated. In Marcilly the houses, gardens, terraces face the Seine instead of turning their backs on it.

I stood on the bridge over the Seine at the confluence of the two rivers, staring at the water, watching la petite Seine emerge blinking into the daylight. It was a moment of great peace, of quiet after Romilly and Troyes and Châtillon. The only sound was the plop of fish. Gradually I began to hear another sound, the sound of music. An old labourer was trudging slowly along the towpath, beret on his head, Gauloise in his mouth, transistor at full blare in his hand. The sound of 'America' grew even louder. As he passed me on the bridge, it was deafening, impossible for us to speak but we nodded at each other. The music stopped abruptly and was replaced by the raucous shout of the disc-jockey. The labourer trudged on into Marcilly, and gradually the silence and the plop of fish seeped back into my consciousness. I went on staring at the river.

Marcilly is charming, one of the prettiest villages on the Seine. Along the river-front is an avenue of limes and behind them an attractive row of eighteenth-century houses – the most pleasing is dated 1736. They were taken over by newly enriched revolutionaries, who wanted to emulate the previous owners, and now they belong to rich Parisians who are fond of shooting and fishing. It was from the window of one of these houses – the one with the octagonal turret – that Claire Deschamps looked out and saw,

with the great flash of love at first sight, the handsome Lord
Bolingbroke.

Claire, Claire de Marcilly as she is called now locally, was in
fact the Marquise de Villette, the young widow of the old marquis, whom she had married soon after leaving school at St Cyr,
where she had acted in Racine with the future Madame de
Maintenon. Viscount Bolingbroke was a Minister of Queen Anne,
but had been banished at the Treaty of Utrecht for being too pro-
French, and was then staying with his friend and fellow-humanist
Voltaire at Sellières nearby. The affair between him and Claire,
first beside the Seine and later beside the Loire, was passionate
indeed, at any rate on Claire's side. When he was pardoned and
returned to England, she wrote him letters in her own blood. In
due course she followed him and, when his wife died, she married
him. They lived in Battersea where, apparently, she was popular
because of her good works, and they are buried there together.
But it is in Marcilly that they are chiefly remembered, if only by
the line of great lime trees, which they planted and which still
stand.

Less happy was the ending for the Gallifret family. The Marquis
de Gallifret was the local aristo, a self-made man who had acquired his fortune from the slave trade. He built his château facing
the confluence of the two rivers, making the most of the fine view.
The château was a copy of Versailles, complete with lakes, gardens, tapis verts, lawns stepped down to the river, orangerie,
Trianon, laiterie and all. So successful was he that Louis XVI came
to stay, with all his court, to the delight of the marquis. Gallifret
was greatly detested locally. Instruments of torture were later
found in his dungeons and the phrase 'malheureux comme un
nègre de Gallifret' is, they say, still heard in the village. In 1793 the
villagers stormed the château and destroyed it stone by stone, and
nothing is now left except part of the orangerie. The marquis fled
and avoided the guillotine. His line did not die out and a des-
cendant distinguished himself during the Franco-Prussian war.
But neither he nor any others have since dared to go back to
Marcilly.

*   *   *   *

Robert Gibbings's charmingly anecdotal *Coming Down the Seine* was my constant companion on this part of the river, and it was Gibbings who led me to the Hotel Beurville at Marcilly. I thought of the hospitable Beurville family, of the pretty daughter Giselle with the black curls and the silver tooth who worked so hard from dawn to dusk, running from the bar to the tables to the petrol pump.

And where, I asked, was Giselle?

They looked at me curiously. Monsieur knows this district well, they ventured.

I tried to explain that I was not exactly a friend of Giselle, but that I had read about her in a book.

In a book? Giselle? They looked at me incredulously. Without doubt I must have read of the hotel in the newspapers. Last year a frogman trying to swim underwater from Troyes to the sea had injured himself at Marcilly and had stayed several days at the hotel. It had been reported in the papers. Look! They produced the cutting.

Eventually I found out about Giselle. She had emigrated to America – what else could the poor girl do? Someone else reported that she now had five children. Monsieur and Madame Beurville had also emigrated – to Rheims, fifty miles away but in the eyes of Marcilly equally far; indeed, even Romilly is regarded there as a distant town. The Hotel Beurville no longer bore that name; it was now, rather coyly, 'Chez Jacqueline'. But the welcome was as warm for me as it had been for Gibbings from Monsieur Beurville and Giselle.

It was really a delightful inn, under the lime trees, facing the Seine. In the stable at the back a trio of acrobats from the Romilly fair was entertaining the village children. The sanitary arrangements in the stable yard were full of character, though, to my distress, it was impossible to reach them after the hotel was locked up for the night at half-past nine.

Gibbings comments on the excellent conversation to be heard in French country bars, the thoughtful observations on art and poetry. Twelve years later he would have found things very changed. The bar at Marcilly was dominated by a large, deafening television set, and the locals came at night, not to discuss Mallarmé but to stand and stare. I do not believe that my host's eyes left the screen for one second during the hours of transmission during my stay there. As the bar was also the dining-room there was no escaping it during meals either. I dined while an elderly man explained at great length how and why he was revising a dictionary. I lunched to the Paris Bourse prices, both written up on a blackboard and read out so that as many senses as possible might be informed. The depressing thing about Bourse prices is that they always seem to be falling, and I was grateful when Jacqueline, who was not addicted to the set, took pity on me and put me alone in a large chilly room normally reserved for wedding receptions.

After dinner, however, I would brave the bar again in search of company, or, if that were not available, just a drink. One night I found someone willing to talk to me. He was an electrical engineer and had been helping to build the new electric power station at Vernou. I must be sure to go and see it, it was très jolie. It had taken five years to build, it was the biggest in the world, it was très jolie. It worked on natural gas which was piped from Bordeaux, that was jolie, it had five hydraulic machines for unloading fifteen trucks of coal a day in case the gas supply broke down, that was jolie too. It had one hundred and twenty kilos de pression, that was vachement jolie.

I had my ear close to his mouth to catch his words. All the time he was speaking, while his right hand conveyed wine to his mouth his eyes never left the screen above my left shoulder, on which giggling ladies in crinolines chased each other round a garden.

Marcilly is in the centre of sugarbeet fields, and when I was there the harvest was just starting. Barges arrived from the sugar factory at Bray further downstream and manoeuvred alongside a quay on the opposite side of the river. Trucks would roar across the bridge and tip their cargo on to the ever-growing heap of sugarbeets on the quay. The actual lifting of the beets from the fields was done by seasonal Breton labour. I talked to some of them one day outside the bar. Yes, they came every year, they said, for two or three months. But this year was not a good year.

'Why not?' I asked.

'The weather is too fine, the earth is too dry. The work will be over too soon.'

I thought it a terribly sad remark. Much jollier was the work of the men driving the mechanical shovels on the quay. In the intervals of loading the barges, they were building the beets into a great mountain beside the river. This, they told me, made the loading much easier. After a certain height the beets spilt on top would just run down the sides of the mountain to the ground, like sand in a child's toy. I could not quite see how it helped the loading, but it must have been fun to do.

I went to call on Madame Virgile Henry, the wife of the Mayor of Marcilly, at her farm. I introduced myself, apologized for troubling her, and said I had been told she might possibly lend me her boat so that I could row on the Seine. I suppose it was rather a surprising request from a total stranger, but she took it in her stride. She had no boat herself, but she was sure her son-in-law would lend me his. She would ask her daughter.

It seemed there was no objection and Madame Henry herself accompanied me out of the farm and along the river bank to show me the boat. I apologized for giving her so much trouble, but she assured me it was no trouble, and she hoped I would have a nice trip and take some good photographs. Could I row, could I swim? I said I had done a good deal of both in my time, but I hoped one would not be necessary.

The boat was moored in a small artificial creek and I man-oeuvred it cautiously into the river. It was one of the days when the Seine was flowing strongly upstream, and I coasted along upstream hardly bothering to pull at the oars. I shot the bridge and when I got opposite Marcilly, I rested on my oars while I tried to photograph Claire's house from the river. Unfortunately I spent too long fiddling with my exposure meter, and during that time the boat drifted upstream faster than I had estimated, past Claire's house. Amused, I pulled lackadaisically on to the confluence with the Aube. It was a lovely autumn day, warm, sunny, but with a stimulating freshness behind the warmth. My thoughts turned agreeably to lunch.

I turned the boat round. It was much harder work coming

downstream and I had to row hard and steadily. I paused for a few seconds to get my picture of Claire's house, and by the time I clipped up the camera case, I was already drifting back towards the Aube. Recalling myself to stern business, reminding myself of the proper sculling technique learned in long hours on the Thames, I got back to the little creek, panting and sweating. I walked back along the bank, flexing my fingers, trying to remember when I had last done any rowing. As I passed the mountain of beets, I remarked to one of the men:

'The Seine is flowing strongly upstream today.'

'Ah bon?' he said discouragingly.

I went on undiscouraged, 'It is without doubt because the Seine does not wish to leave France and arrive in the Channel'.

'Ah bon?' he said again.

I fear there is a less fey explanation of the phenomenon. Though the Seine has many weirs and locks, they are very shallow. The total drop between the sources and the sea is only 470 metres, and most of this takes place in the Côte d'Or when the Seine is still only a trickle. There are no snow mountains to give spates in the spring, and the tributaries are all equally gentle. The Seine is in consequence a very slow meandering river; even at its full width, at Rouen, it only reaches an average of five hundred cubic metres of water a second (compare the Danube's nine thousand). It is, as nearly as such a thing exists, a stationary river and the slightest breeze is enough to move the surface of the water downwind, upstream. And with a winding river like the Seine, every breeze blows upstream somewhere.

I went into the farm to report the safe return of the boat and to thank Madame Henry once again. She was standing in her farmyard, under a big cart, surrounded by alarming dogs and unalarmed chickens. She looked so charming that I asked if I might photograph her too. This worried her; she wanted to go and change her dress and do her hair. But I begged her not to. I wanted her just as she was, in her blue frock and her pink apron, under the shafts of her cart, laughing.

So I photographed her like that, the embodiment of human friendliness.

15

The weather had broken by the time I reached Nogent. It was raining hard, and the wind, still upstream, was strong enough to blow my umbrella inside out as I stood on the bridge. Nogent is dominated by the huge flour mills which straddle the Seine like a barracks on a bridge. I stood beside them and watched, on the other side of the river, a youth beating up a smaller boy with shocking savagery. He threw the boy down a flight of stone steps, picked him up and hurled him against a wall like a ball, and kicked him, taking a good run each time. The boy screamed for help, I shouted and waved my extraordinary umbrella, the woman beside me said, 'C'est méchant, ça.' A few feet away from the boys, the lavoir was full of washerwomen scrubbing their clothes. Armed with their scrubbing brushes, they would have been formidable guardians of the peace, but they kept their heads down, resolutely seeing and hearing nothing. The boy, surprisingly, was not killed. At least, both he and his assailant had disappeared by the time I reached the place. But it was a stark Dickensian scene, in the driving rain, under the dark bulk of the mill.

Despite this unpromising start, I found Nogent a pleasant old town. There are villas beside the Seine, chestnuts, picturesque corners, old houses. Henri IV had a hunting and loving lodge there; it still stands, a rambling half-timbered cottage incongruously sited nowadays in a factory yard. Napoleon was also there twice during the campaign of 1814, but he was too busy for boars or women. Another building I liked was the Hotel du Cygne de la Croix, built around a courtyard and at one time a convent. I asked about the name and was duly told about the swan with a cross on its head. But personally I suspect that the pun came first and that someone thought up the legend later.

Nogent was originally a fortified town and the church too was strongly fortified. Indeed, it seems now more a castle than a church. On top of its tower is a great enlarged replica of St

Lawrence's gridiron, which, to my mind, adds to the building's interest rather than beauty. Louis XIV, however, held the opposite view and renamed the town Nogent La Belle Tour.

Nogent used to be the first river port above Paris, and full of sailors and barge-horses. In 1450 a statue of a girl, with a very beautiful expression, was found in the river and placed in a chapel. Known as La Belle Dame, she was for over three hundred years an object of pilgrimage, particularly for sailors, until one day, shortly before the Revolution, someone threw her back into the Seine. She is, of course, assumed to have been a Virgin, but I felt that she was more likely to have been another version of my old friend Sequana.

Equally an object of pilgrimage, though of a more secular kind, and today equally invisible, is the convent Le Paraclet, founded by Abelard and of which Héloïse was the first abbess. I did not visit it as there is now nothing to be seen except the tomb in which their bodies may have rested for a time.

The story of Héloïse and Abelard is one that never seems to die. Year after year new versions of it appear in the bookshops; and indeed the story of that ill-starred love is, despite its medievalism and churchiness, truly modern in its feeling of frustration, its double standards and its Freudian overtones. The villain of the piece is usually acknowledged to be Canon Fulbert, Héloïse's uncle and guardian. Personally I think it was the character of Abelard himself that was so damaging.

Abelard's qualities are well known: his physical beauty, his voice, his songs, his eloquence, his scholarship, his argumentativeness, his subtlety. In more Christian qualities such as self-abnegation, humility, charity or chastity he was notably lacking. It was taken for granted, by Abelard as well as by everyone else, that he was destined for a glorious career in the church, though it is far from clear why, when he first met Héloïse, he was still not a priest though he was approaching middle age. For a man of God he was singularly complacent and unrepentant about his seducing of Héloïse, his teenage pupil, and indeed there is no reason to believe that she was his first. There are hints of promiscuity in his letters and at one point he taunts poor Héloïse with all the women he might have had but for her – 'I feared no refusal from whatever woman I might deem worthy of my love'. His wish to keep his marriage secret from the world and the church was less than frank. And his dumping his young wife, the mother of his son, in a convent for ever, in the interests of his career, was hardly the action of a great lover.

Of course, to be awakened in your bedroom late at night by thugs hired by your wife's uncle, and castrated, must be a depressing experience for any man, particularly for one as vain and sexual as Abelard. He was very sorry for himself, and with good reason. But there is no sign that he was ever the least bit sorry for Héloïse whom he had already condemned to a lifetime of nunneries, for which she admitted she had no vocation. Indeed, it seems that from the moment when she tiresomely became pregnant, he was fed up with her.

To become the great love story, the perfect romance, the story needs careful editing, and I was amused by the illustrated version which hung in the lobby of my hotel in Nogent. The first picture showed the couple being introduced, she tall, fair and wimpled, he dark, bearded and equally young. Later scenes showed them walking together in gardens; Héloïse listening to Abelard singing, while the wicked uncle hovered in the background. The final picture showed them both kneeling before Canon Fulbert, being joined in holy wedlock. There the story ends, though an unillustrated line of print at the bottom of the page mentions that later Abelard was attacked by men hired by the Canon and received wounds from which he died. In fact, far from being the young bridegroom, Abelard was thirty-nine when he was mutilated, and he lived to the age of sixty-three, writing patronizing letters to Héloïse and controversial treatises on the impossibility of a *nomen* also being a *res*.

Their bodies do not now lie in Nogent. After the Revolution they were cremated and buried in Père Lachaise, united not only in death but in their joint indestructible love for Peter Abelard.

16

'A beautiful name and an even more beautiful reality!' Such is Michelin's poetic description of the Île-de-France. The 'island' is bounded by five rivers, the Yonne, the Eure, the Epte, the Aisne and the Marne. Across it, dividing the island into two, flows the Seine; in the middle of it is Paris. It would be invidious to assert that this is the most beautiful landscape in France or indeed to compare it with other regions. Certainly it has some lovely parts, especially in the river valleys. Elsewhere it may perhaps seem flat and monotonous; plains divided geometrically by straight roads and lines of poplars, less spectacular than other regions, other provinces. But the Île-de-France is beyond doubt the heart of France. Here was the ancient kingdom of the Franks, of King Clovis and Hugues Capet. Here was the beginning of France, to which everything else, duchies, counties, provinces, was later added.

We enter the Île-de-France at Montereau; Montereau-fault-Yonne, the point at which the Yonne falls into the Seine. Not that there are any falls at that point. Both rivers run smoothly and slowly, the Seine brown and fairly clear, the Yonne green and thick. The Yonne seemed slightly the larger; indeed, there are those who, ignoring Sequana, claim that the Yonne is the true Seine.

The bridges over both rivers were destroyed, like almost all the others on the Seine outside Paris, in 1944. These had been replaced by temporary iron bridges, which were now in turn being replaced by exceptionally fine modern bridges. The one over the Yonne is completed, the one over the Seine still under construction. It was in the middle of the Yonne bridge in 1419 that Jean Sans Peur, Duke of Burgundy, met the Dauphin, the future Charles VII, to arrange an alliance against the English. In the middle of the discussions the duke's head was split open by one of the knights accompanying the Dauphin. This act of treachery made the Burgundians return to their alliance with the English and brought about directly the Treaty of Troyes, which made Henry v of England Regent of France. Duke Philip, the son of Jean Sans Peur, captured the town and punished it severely. In 1437 Charles vii recaptured it and hanged the Burgundian supporters. It was a bloody time for Montereau.

Napoleon was also there. In February 1814 he won one of his last battles against the allies, throwing back the Austrians under Schwarzenberg with a brilliance that recalled his earlier days. It was on this occasion that he reassured his troops with his famous remark, 'The bullet which will kill me has not yet been made'. Unfortunately for him he wasted his victory. He wrote a full account of his future plans to the Empress, and the messenger carrying the letter was captured by the allies, who made good use of this intelligence.

There is a statue of the Emperor, sculpted by the son of the general who had commanded the cavalry in the battle, at the point of confluence of the two rivers. But the 'island', when I saw it, was a mass of cement, sand, corrugated iron, steel rods, backing lorries, bulldozers, all part of the rebuilding of the Seine bridge.

I asked a workman, 'Where is Napoleon?'

He pointed at a box of corrugated iron. 'In Elba.'

Montereau life moves on several levels. Leaving my hotel in the morning I noticed the local bowls club having a formal meeting. At midday they adjourned for a long and rather expensive lunch. Afterwards they resumed their meeting and continued in session till late in the evening. Sport is evidently a serious business in Montereau.

There are two pleasant leafy squares in the town, full of humble restaurants, frequented by men I took to be humble commercial travellers humbly eating soup in a decor which reminded me irresistibly of an Eastbourne boarding house – oak dresser, china ducks, plastic birds, brown wallpaper and lino. Montereau is a busy port and down on the Quai de l'Yonne I found the café where the bargees rush in, collect their mail, gulp down a glass of wine and rush out again. Bargees are always in a hurry.

They were rebuilding the concrete lavoir beside the Seine, and I strolled in to look at it. Why were they rebuilding it, I asked, thinking of all the launderettes in the town, all the shops selling washing machines. Was it much used still?

Certainly it was, I was told, more so than ever now that the town was bigger. The damp concrete floor sloped down to the river in order to accommodate varying heights of the Seine. Kneeling downhill, scrubbing clothes in the cold polluted water, I wondered if any more uncomfortable way of washing clothes could be devised. And yet, despite the town's prosperity, it was worthwhile rebuilding the lavoir. Montereau, I decided, was an intriguing blend of the ancient and the modern.

The town is growing fast. The idea is to extend its port, so as to take the strain and the congestion off Paris. Its industries – sugar, bricks, agricultural machinery – will be immensely expanded now that it has been declared an industrial zone. But the most exciting project is the new town of Surville, beside the château where Napoleon had his headquarters.

Surville stands on a plateau overlooking the Seine valley, with wide wonderful views. It can therefore be seen from a long stretch of the river, a white city on a hill, a dream of a new Jerusalem. I greatly admired the planning and the architecture of the buildings, the clean lines and shapes, the judicious use of colour, the sense of landscape and variety. For the buildings are not monotonous; each one is significantly different. Some are long and low, some tall and slender. The tallest, not yet completed, will have twenty-five floors. Even the water-tower and the chimney of the boiler-house have been turned into graceful vertical features. All it seemed at first sight to lack was a garden scheme worthy of the rest.

When finished it will have, I was told, six thousand flats, a population of twenty to twenty-five thousand people. It has its own shopping centre, its own school, its own football ground. The central heating, the hot water for six thousand bathrooms, is provided centrally and included in the rent.

'Yes, it is very convenient,' a woman told me, while she queued for vegetables. 'And not expensive.'

It took me a little while to spot what was wrong, what was

missing. There were no cafés! This was no accident. There was no
provision for cafés, it was not intended there should be any, it was
part of the fight against alcohol. Imagine a town of twenty thousand Frenchmen, and no café! Nowhere to go for a cup of coffee,
nowhere to meet your friends. And it is not only cafés that are
missing in Surville. Apart from the school and the football
ground, there are no communal meeting places, no hall, no
church, no cinema, and no provision for them.

'What do you do in the evening?' I asked my informant.

'Rien!'

'What do you do at week-ends?'

'Rien!'

'Why don't you complain then?'

She shrugged. 'One grows accustomed to it.'

In fact, the population of Surville goes down into Montereau
by the regular bus service and uses the cafés there. So they are
pulling down the pretty little square of cafés beside the Seine in
the interests of road-widening. I expect they will discontinue the
bus service next.

The intention is that every family should spend its spare time at
home in its own flat, watching television. Personally I expect there
to be a great deal of crime there in the years ahead. Surville is
wonderful to look at, wonderful to look from, but I for one am
glad that I do not have to live there.

17

Below Montereau the Seine is a broad, open river, now officially
la haute Seine and no longer la petite Seine. On the right bank is a
line of low hills, on the other the alluvial plain. The road follows
the right bank, there are railways on both, pylons march across
the plain. On my left was suddenly an enormous building with
two tall chimneys. Pylons and chimneys – it suddenly dawned on
me that this was the jolie Centrale d'Electricité my friend in
Marcilly had described to me.

Seizing my suitcase, I asked the bus driver to stop, and we shuddered to a halt. I found myself on the side of the road, separated from the power-station by the railway, which was fenced off. Surprisingly there seemed to be no entrance, no gate, no keeper. But on closer inspection I found a small tunnel, wired and defended, with a notice stating that unauthorized entry was strictly forbidden. The gate, however, was ajar. I searched again for some more approved entry, but again I found nothing. Hiding my suitcase in some bushes under a tree, feeling rather like James Bond, I crept down the steps into the tunnel.

The tunnel was long and straight, lit at intervals by lamps. I was acutely aware that, if I were suddenly set upon by Doberman Pinschers or attacked by Koreans with grenades, I should find it difficult to take cover. But the tunnel was deserted, the only sound my tiptoe footsteps. At the far end, at the top of the steps, the gate was also open; and I slid out into daylight. I was in the main yard of the Centrale and in the distance was a uniformed gate-keeper. Shaking off my furtiveness, I marched boldly up to him and said 'Bonjour'.

He looked at me suspiciously. 'How did you come in?'

I said vaguely, 'Par le chemin'.

'You did not enter by the tunnel?'

'Well, er, yes.'

'Then you must go out again and return through the proper entrance. It is two kilometres down the road.'

This seemed to me a dismal idea. I asked to see Monsieur le Directeur.

'Have you an appointment?'

I produced my card. 'I am sure he will be glad to see me.'

A few minutes later I found myself sitting in the office of the Directeur-Adjoint. He did not say that he was delighted to meet me as he had always been interested in studying the limits of human pain. But he seemed pleased enough. I suppose I was a welcome interruption, a foreigner out of the blue, a writer wanting to know all about his beautiful Centrale. He snowed me with maps, statistics, pictures of the inside of turbines, diagrams of electrical circuits.

No, it was not the largest in the world, but it was at the moment the largest in France. It supplied electricity to the European grid, même à l'Angleterre. It had been started in 1956 and since then its production had been tripled. It now had four turbines with a total output of 750,000 kilowatts. The temperature of the steam reached 568 degrees Centigrade. Water from the Seine was used for cooling, and afterwards was returned to the river.

Yes, indeed, it ran on natural gas from Lacq, near Pau in the Pyrenees. The gas came by subterranean pipe, passing under the Loire as well as the Seine. But now the gas, being clean and safe, was being diverted to the kitchens of Paris and the Centrale would work on 'less noble' fuel, coal. But there was oil in the forest, a refinery only twenty kilometres away, and soon the Centrale would run on fuel oil. All fuels, it seemed, were the same to it.

The Centrale was fully automated. Coal arriving by railway truck was transferred to the boilers without the need of any human intervention. And later, walking through the Centrale, my impression was one of cavernous emptiness. The great turbines spun quietly; far above me, like the sky, was the roof. A few workmen stood about looking at dials, like bored tourists in an empty cathedral. For all the thousands of kilowatts humming round me, it was a very peaceful place.

18

A few hundred yards from the Centrale d'Electricité, within sight of the chimneys, almost within their shadow, we take a dizzy jump back seventeen thousand years. Not far from the underground gas pipe from the Pyrenees is Pincevent, once the best ford across the Seine; and there the reindeer crossed the river each year during the final centuries of the last ice age; and there the Magdalenian men waited to hunt them.

The Seine has changed its course a little since then, and during the last two centuries it has become deep. There is no ford now

in those parts, and Pincevent is today a wilderness of sand excavations and artificial lakes. But recently there was discovered
there the remains of a Magdalenian camp, unique in Western
Europe.

We know a little of the life and art of Palaeolithic man in his
caves. But such life was exceptional – as rare as the caves themselves. Normal life was in the open, in temporary camps, and
traces of these have disappeared into the earth they occupied so
briefly. The significance of Pincevent is that it shows us for the
first time just how they lived in the open. The site was abandoned
when in full use, apparently at very short notice, and was
preserved undisturbed until its discovery in 1964.

The Magdalenian tribe would come once a year to Pincevent,
lured both by the reindeer and by the chalk cliff on the right bank
of the Seine, a fruitful source of crude flints. While they waited
for the reindeer they would pitch their camp by the ford, meticu-
lously in lines like army tents. Each man would sit about six feet
from his neighbour on a large stone in front of his hearth, chipping
raw flints, surrounded by chalk and debris. The hearths were
about twenty centimetres deep and forty centimetres across, filled
with bones and charcoal and cinders, and they were surrounded
with stones to conserve and radiate the heat. The heat was enough
to explode the stones, though it must have seemed little enough in
that frozen age.

When the reindeer herd arrived, they would be hunted and the
tribe would settle to an orgy of venison. Stews were cooked by
putting hot stones into reindeer-skin containers. The place would
be a mass of reindeer bones covering the new flints. It was occupied only a few weeks in the year; the tribe would move off,
carrying their meat, their antlers and their new supply of flints,
roaming Europe – for at that time there was no Channel, no
North Sea. The following year they, or another tribe, would be
back at Pincevent.

Magdalenian man was a nomad, a hunter. The idea of staying in
one place, of farms and crops and livestock, did not come till the
ice age receded into history. We know that the Pincevent camp
was occupied every year for several centuries until the climate

grew too warm for reindeer, and they changed their habits, look-ing for colder grazing further north. What happened in the cen-turies before Magdalenian man we do not know, as the changing course of the Seine has washed away all vestiges.

It is fascinating to imagine our shaggy ancestors sitting there beside the Seine, chipping and waiting. What extraordinary people they must have been to survive at all in such an odious climate. In this century it is considered a fine feat of courage to shoot a rhinoceros or an elephant with a precision rifle. To tackle a rhinoceros, a bison or a mammoth, equipped only with a flint axe or a harpoon made of reindeer antlers, must have required courage of quite a different order, the courage perhaps of desperation.

What made them abandon the Pincevent camp so abruptly is uncertain. It had been occupied only briefly; the flint blades were still new, the debris untrampled. They left, taking with them only the antlers and the worked bones – for none of these were found at the site. The precious flints, the burins, they left behind. It could not have been a hostile tribe or there would have been traces of the fight, tramplings, and the victors would surely have taken away the new flints. It could have been a storm threatening floods, heavy enough to cause them to break camp and covering every-thing with thick clay mud; but not violent enough to wash away the bones and the debris in a torrent.

The site at Pincevent covers at least a hectare. Only three hearths have so far been completely excavated and much of the rest has been churned about by the sand-dredgers. The site was occupied long after the Magdalenian men went away. Farms grew up beside the ford as the climate grew more temperate. The traces of Magdalenian man were buried deep in the mud, but in layers above them the excavators have unearthed an enormous quantity of relics of later civilizations – polished axes and pottery from the Neolithic age, bronze daggers, iron, Gallic coins, Roman ceramics, the remains of a Roman villa. Layer upon layer of history, from mammoths to pylons, all on the same site.

*   *   *   *

The local expert was Madame Roux, the young and pretty wife of the doctor in La Grande Paroisse, the next village. It was she who had saved the site from the sand-dredgers and who had summoned the experts from Paris; and it was she who kindly showed me photographs and papers and explained the importance of the find.

Yet more palaeolithic flints and bones would not in themselves have been an exciting discovery. The significance of Pincevent was in their precise position. Nothing must be moved until it had all been measured and photographed. It was a very difficult dig, as the bones were far more brittle than the clay which had preserved them. It took three thousand working hours, spent mostly kneeling on planks above the site, to uncover the thousands of vestiges of three hearths alone. In the middle of it all a storm covered everything, within a few hours, with three or four inches of mud – perhaps a repeat performance of the original crisis which had driven out the Magdalenian tribe.

It was a sunny autumn day when Madame Roux told me about it. Her sitting-room looked across the Seine valley, and it hummed with Mozart, a sewing-machine and small burbling children. Record-players, tweeds, archaeology – how typical of the mid-twentieth century! The reindeer seemed every minute of those seventeen thousand years away.

19

I arrived at Madame Roux's house in a car belonging to the Centrale d'Electricité, having introduced myself a few minutes earlier on the telephone from the office of the Directeur-Adjoint. The car was driven by my old friend, the uniformed gate-keeper, who was by now looking at me rather queerly. First he had apprehended me making an unauthorized entry into the Centrale, then he had conducted me to a private interview with the management, and now he was driving me in a hurry to the doctor.

Would he mind stopping the car for a moment, I asked, as I wished to collect my suitcase hidden under that tree?

He gave me a terribly brave smile.

I continued my journey from La Grande Paroisse, however, in my familiar bus, past the Centrale and the tunnel entrance, past Vernou, to Saint-Mammès.

Saint-Mammès stands at the point where the Seine is joined by another tributary, the Loing, and Sisley painted a famous picture of it, now in the Jeu de Paume. Incredibly, the village has not changed at all since Sisley's day, except for a few small details: there are more barges now – Sisley only painted three. The trees have grown up along the river, the bridge was destroyed in the war and replaced by a temporary one. But Saint-Mammès is still the same, a delightful string of small red-roofed dolls' houses along the waterfront.

I was now in Impressionist country and from here to the sea it was impossible not to be aware of it at every turn. It was like having someone constantly beside you saying, 'This is how it should look, this is how it really looks'. The Seine dominated the lives of so many of those painters and now by a natural philosophic reversal, it is they who dominate the Seine, just as Shakespeare irretrievably dominated and altered the character of a probably jolly, extrovert Danish prince. Is the Seine at Saint-Mammès really as blue, as wide as that? Is the sky really as huge, as luminous? Of course it is. To wander at will down the Seine should be sufficient pleasure for any man. But to feel that you are strolling, sailing, drinking, top-hatted, frock-coated, through a series of Impressionist paintings immeasurably increases that enjoyment.

Saint-Mammès is an important port and refuelling point for barges. Both waterfronts, the Seine and the Loing, are lined with them four or six deep, flying their washing like bunting at a regatta. Every house seems to be a shop catering for their needs; chandlers, grocers, cafés, all run by retired bargees. For all happy bargees hope to go to Saint-Mammès when they retire.

I had intended to stay at Saint-Mammès, but, alas, there was no room for me at any of the inns. Who could be occupying their bedrooms I could not imagine, for no true bargee would dream of sleeping ashore even if the accommodation were free. So I was forced to go to Moret, a mile up the Loing.

This, as it turned out, was far from being a penance, for Moret is delightful. On the left bank of the Loing, on the edge of the Forest of Fontainebleau, Moret is a small old walled town, full of old winding streets, old houses, towers, dungeons, trees. Many historical personages have been there, behaving characteristically: Thomas à Becket excommunicating, Francois I hunting, Henri IV loving, Napoleon planning new campaigns, Sisley painting. But, unlike Troyes, Moret is not falling down. The citizens of Moret take trouble in looking after the treasure around them and in catering discreetly for the tourist. Of course Moret is much smaller; you can walk round it in a morning, drive round it in a few minutes. But it has good hotels and restaurants – I ate an excellent steak au poivre looking out at the dark waters of the Loing. In summer it even has son et lumière.

None of this is rammed at you; Moret takes its attractions in its stride. You are aware that the chief interest of the place now is not tourism but fishing. Dozens of shops cater for this sport and over my breakfast I watched the banks of the river flickering with rods even though it was a weekday morning. The Loing, they say, has the best fishing in France. I do not know. It is certainly a very pretty river, smaller than the Seine, with its lawns and trees a little more artificial, a river for recreation rather than for commerce.

On the far bank was a solitary neo-Sisley among the fishermen. He was painting the most photographed and painted view of Moret across the river. I wandered round and looked at his Impressionist landscape. Moret certainly is well composed from this point, the big old church with its flying buttresses, the dungeon, the old houses, the trees, the bridge. Sisley, who lived in Moret for more than twenty years, painted this view. But personally I do not think it among his best pictures. Perhaps it was too pretty for him, perhaps there was too little water, too little sky for his purposes.

I could have lingered for a considerable time in Moret, but my business lay with the Seine. So I retraced my steps to the greater river, the bustle of Saint-Mammès. I went into a quayside café for a glass of wine, and an enormously fat bargee, sitting in his vest, raised his glass to me in welcome.

It was time, I decided, that I found out more about the barge life of the Seine. I approached the smartly painted barge *Sacolève* which was refuelling and hailed its owner. Would it be possible for me to take a voyage on his barge?

Of course! He was leaving in five minutes. Come aboard!

Only when we were out in the stream did I bother to ask where we were going, not that it mattered.

'Montereau.'

Well, why not? I was getting to know that stretch of the Seine, but now I was seeing it through the eyes not of an electrical engineer or an archaeologist, but a bargee. It made quite a different picture. For instance, I learned that the barges lining the banks were immovable, houseboats, the homes of retired bargees who could not bear to leave the river.

The river life is a world of its own and is kept carefully insulated from the outer world. My host, Monsieur Lenoir, had been born on a barge; so had his wife, who came up the stairs to welcome me. His four children – two boys away at boarding school, two engaging small girls Lydie and Michèle sitting on the shelf behind the steering wheel – had all been born on board an earlier barge. The next child (due, it seemed to me, at any minute) would be born on *Sacolève*, and this would bring the barge good luck. So, no doubt, would later children.

I stood beside Monsieur Lenoir while he steered the barge and talked to me. Madame, having greeted me, went down to the cabin to continue cooking. The girls giggled on their shelf; when not on the shelf they were tied to a hook in the wheelhouse to prevent them falling downstairs or overboard. There was also a cat called Minou, a dog trained to sit quietly under the steering wheel, a flock of chickens in the sand in the hold. It was a very happy family.

They were all terribly houseproud and the place was immaculate. There were plants in the wheelhouse, carpet in the cabin. All the wooden surfaces were polished or varnished. Monsieur Lenoir stood on a gleaming wooden platform to steer, carefully taking off his shoes first. There were two cookers, one outside for smoky work like frying; a refrigerator working on diesel; an electric generator for the lights. He did not himself have television, but many barges did.

It was the same in the cabin. It is of course essential to be tidy when living in cramped conditions, but this was something far and away beyond that. Off the cabin were the sleeping quarters, two cupboards with portholes, each entirely filled by a double bed. It was here that the baby would be born, an arrangement which the Lenoirs regarded with delight, though personally I thought it might pose problems for the midwife.

Bargees like large families. Monsieur Lenoir, to his sorrow, had only one sister, and she was a nun. But Madame was one of seven and had plenty of relations. And they all marry each other. Very rarely a son might marry a fille de terre, but a daughter would never marry away from the river. The Lenoirs seemed to be related to every bargee on the Seine. All the way it was, 'Voilà, encore un cousin' and we would all wave and Madame would come up from the cabin to wave too. But I wondered how the boys courted the girls in these conditions. Was it done entirely by waving from one barge to another? During short hurried meetings in locks? Odd half-hours while both barges happened to be in Saint-Mammès together? Anyway it seemed to work well, for the race seemed in no danger of dying out.

We were passing the Centrale d'Electricité once more and I opened the wheelhouse door to photograph that familiar building from the river side. My hands were full of exposure meters and filters, and at this moment Michèle suddenly gave me all her rubber balls. It was a princely, if temporary, gift, but it did make photography more difficult. Madame put her head up the stairs to see what the unusual courant d'air was, so I hastily shut the door again.

There is something exhilarating about a growing prosperous industry. The water traffic on the Seine was expanding all the time; over the past three years it had grown by about a quarter each year, I was told. There was plenty of work for everyone; six to eight hundred boats, including Sacolève, were carrying sand from Montereau to Paris for the rebuilding and refacing now going on in and round the capital.

Monsieur Lenoir made enough to send his children to boarding school. But he worked hard for it.

Did he work at night too, I asked.

No, only on the Basse-Seine below Rouen. Or exceptionally when the locks were very crowded. But normally he worked from six in the morning till eight at night, every day including Sundays.

Did he ever take a holiday?

He laughed at that. Look, he owned his own barge and so he would be paying for it himself, wouldn't he? Just the five compulsory public holidays in the year: Christmas, Easter, the first of May, the fourteenth of July and the eleventh of November. I could see that even those rankled with him. Oh, and ten days after the birth of a child, he added, until his wife could help him again.

We were passing the desolate sand-pits of Pincevent, and I thought of telling him about the reindeer and the working life of his Magdalenian ancestors. But I thought better of it. I didn't want to change the subject and anyway we were all facing the opposite way, waving at another cousin.

Monsieur Lenoir's great interest was the other barges on the river; it was his social life. He carried sand, this cousin carried coal, that cousin carried sugar from Bray or flour from Nogent. Other barges, for once unrelated, brought oil from the refinery at Vernou to Rouen and Le Havre. But he carried sand, two hundred and eighty tons of it at a time, and it cost no more to move than a lorry-load. He made a separate contract for each trip, and he never stayed more than an hour anywhere if he could help it. Half a day for the turn round was his maximum stay anywhere.

Half the fleet was like *Sacolève*, owner-occupied, and it was there that most of the friends and cousins were. The other half were owned by the big companies like Sablières or Morillon-Corvol, and he was a little suspicious of these. The companies were now buying pousseurs – powerful tugs which pushed a solid block of four or six barges locked two abreast in front of them. It was a far cry from the tug pulling a long string of barges in Renoir's picture, and it seemed a negation of the basic principle of nautical design, that of sharp end at the front. However, it does save a lot of manpower; in a string of barges, every barge has to be steered separately.

The pousseurs made an enormous wash and noise as they passed. 'It's worse than television,' commented Monsieur Lenoir. We gazed closely as they passed by, but we did not wave.

'Private owners cannot afford to buy pousseurs like that,' he said sadly. 'They have eight hundred horsepower and they can carry two thousand tons each journey.' Then he brightened again. 'But that is much too big for the small contracts.'

He cut his speed as we approached the lock and there was much shouting from cousins emerging from the lock about the queue ahead of us. We were in luck, the gates were open, there was only one barge in front. Madame emerged and went forward to help with the mooring. It struck me, watching her balancing along the narrow rim between the hold and the river, grappling with hawsers, that she was in no condition for that sort of thing, and for one idiotic moment I almost offered to help. The moment the engine stopped Monsieur Lenoir darted below for his lunch. Five minutes later he was back again, his meal finished.

'Always in a hurry,' he said, laughing.

A few minutes later we were coming out of the lock. Madame went below again. Ahead of us on the hill was Surville, shining in the October sunshine, looking more like the New Jerusalem than ever.

Monsieur Lenoir was saying to me that soon he would be a sort of a pousseur too. He had enough horsepower to push another barge in front of his own. That was impossible now, he would be obliged by law to take on two paid hands and to pay their National Insurance contributions. But when they were fourteen his boys would leave school and come to work for him, and then he would buy a second barge. He would not then have to take on extra hands and he would not have to pay insurance contributions for his boys. He rubbed his hands at the prospect. The boys, I presumed, would hardly set foot ashore for the rest of their lives.

We parted on the quay at Montereau. There was no time for a drink together or anything like that. I thanked them all for the voyage and their company, and I promised to send them photographs of themselves and the barge.

'Next time you see *Sacolève* at a quay,' said Monsieur Lenoir, 'you must be sure to come and see us. And écoutez! Remember now you have friends everywhere on the river. Just tell them you have been with us on *Sacolève* and you will be welcome.'

I said, 'Now I too have cousins everywhere'.

They laughed at that. 'Voilà!'

20

It felt quite like home, being back in Montereau again, and the first person I ran into was Madame Roux, shopping.

'Tiens! I thought you were a long way away by now, down the river.'

'I was,' I said, 'but I've come back. I've just stepped off a barge. And I've seen Pincevent. Electricity, reindeer, barges, what a combination!'

She laughed. 'Voilà! That's the Seine.'

I was too late for lunch so I went into a café for cheese and wine.

Certainly, Madame la patronne said, and she was happy to recommend me particularly her Beaujolais which was very good and a speciality of the place.

I was delighted to agree. The clean shiny bottle was brought to me reverently in a cradle, as if it were Corton or Chambertin, carefully uncorked, gently poured. It was remarkably unlike Beaujolais, pink, fizzy, leaving a thick brown sediment at the bottom of the glass. The label announced proudly that it was Beaujolais 1959. Another label revealed that it had been selected, matured and bottled in the establishment.

The elderly waitress was hovering about at a loose end, so I asked her about it. Did they really bottle all their own wine?

'Yes, indeed,' she said. They were lucky in having big cellars. The wine came from the growers in barrels and they bottled it themselves. That was why it was particularly good.

Yes indeed, I said, particularly good! But was there anything to stop them putting in some other wine and calling it Beaujolais – not that they ever did such a thing of course.

Nothing, she agreed cheerfully. But of course they only put the best Beaujolais into their bottles. They had an arrangement with the grower. That was why it was so particularly good.

'Particularly good,' I echoed. I was aware of the patronne, hovering about unhappily behind me, trying to catch the waitress's eye. But she was too interested discussing wine with me to notice.

Some of the wholesalers, she was saying, did terrible things. They would buy any wine, French, Spanish, Algerian, anything, mix it all together and sell it as Beaujolais. But never in this house, of course. That was why their wine was so particularly good.

'Evidemment,' I said, sipping cautiously.

The patronne was buzzing with misery behind me, emptying ashtrays, kicking my chair, waving at the waitress. But I held her with my glittering eye.

'But surely,' I said, 'Beaujolais is an appellation controlée. It says so there on the label.'

The waitress shrugged. 'How can you test taste? You can test the alcohol and the acidity, but taste –'

The patronne behind me said, 'Thérèse –'

I interrupted her. 'So I must remember only to drink Beaujolais here. But tell me, is it the same with the great wines, the great Burgundies, Corton, Nuits-St Georges, Pommard?'

'Ah no, that is a little different. The growers send inspectors round to taste the wine. We do not know who they are.'

'Me, perhaps,' I offered.

She shook her head. 'Pas un Anglais. And the growers only issue exactly the right number of labels for the bottles. You cannot get spare labels of Pommard.'

'Ah,' I said.

'Anyway the clients would know. Someone who orders Pommard would know if he were being given something else.'

There it was again, the theory I had often heard in France: that the only reason a man orders Beaujolais at six francs a bottle rather than Pommard at twenty-six is because he cannot tell one wine from another, and therefore need not be given even Beaujolais for his money.

'Thank you,' I said to the waitress, releasing her. 'It's very interesting.'

The patronne promptly swept her away into the kitchen.

I continued my journey by my familiar bus. The driver, in fact, recognized me.

'To the Centrale d'Electricité?'

'Not today. Further.'

'Well, where are you going to, then?'

'I don't know.' I hesitated, wondering what was the French for 'How do I know where I'm going till I get there?' 'Champagne-sur-Seine,' I said, largely because it was a jolly name.

But Champagne, when I got there, was by no means a jolly place, industrialized, with its back turned to the river, and I continued to Thoméry, to the bewilderment of the driver.

Thoméry has a small plage beside the Seine where sun-seekers from Fontainebleau come at week-ends to display their bikinis and occasionally to swim. But Thoméry is chiefly known for its grapes. Indeed, from the descriptions, I had imagined every house to be covered with trellises and vines. But in fact most of the houses are faced with the usual roughcast cement, and trellises are rare, and then usually without vines. The vines do still exist, however, in gardens and courtyards, on inside, south-facing walls. The grapes are cut in the autumn and taken to special chambres des raisins which are kept at an exact temperature and degree of humidity. The bunches are put in vases of water, for all the world as if they were flowers, and they keep in perfect condition till the following April or May. This technique had been discovered in 1848 by a local vine-grower who had wished to present some specially fine bunches to the patron saint of vine-growers, Saint Vincent, whose day had been tiresomely fixed for January.

The patronne of the bar on which I was leaning seemed very bored with the grapes. The owners of the chambres des raisins were very jaloux and women were not allowed in the store-rooms.

'Why not?' I asked.

Well, women carried the curse of Eve and so they would turn the grapes sour, naturellement. She shrugged. She had been in Thoméry nineteen years and had never seen any grapes yet.

The industry, it seemed, was on the decline. It was all a great deal of bother and expense, and the rather limited demand for grapes in January, Saint Vincent notwithstanding, is now catered for by imports from the other hemisphere.

A woman came into the bar. Her car had broken down outside. Could Madame la patronne possibly change her a franc so that she might telephone a garage. Madame firmly shook her head. No, she had absolutely no change in the house, not even for a franc. I fished in my pocket and found the right number of centimes, which I gave to the lady who accepted them gratefully. When she had gone Madame said, if she started giving change, she would have to give it to everyone, wouldn't she.

She was closing the bar as she spoke, although it was still very early. It was all right for me, she said, but she had to be up in time to open the bar at six to serve rum and cognac to labourers on their way to work.

Cursed or not, I thought she was enough to send any grapes sour.

At first sight the restaurant of my small hotel seemed to be a little-known haven of gluttony. It boasted a special menu gastronomique and the table was littered with such works as *Larousse Gastronomique, l'Art Culinaire, Cuisine et Vins de France*. All, however, was illusion. The menu gastronomique was not on that night and Madame la patronne, I discovered later, was unable to read. So I dined à la française, steak and chips and television.

It was a meal I seemed to have eaten twice a day since I left Burgundy, the staple fare of every French inn between Troyes and Charenton, and, I have no doubt, of many other areas besides. There are of course the famous restaurants, the bonnes tables, Michelin-starred, but these are only for tourists and for the wine-and-food correspondents of the British Sunday papers. There are, equally, less pretentious places, but still catering for tourists and having a chef and kitchen staff, where you will be offered a good variety of dishes. Such had been my restaurant in Moret. But in the ordinary French country inn where Madame does the cooking herself you must expect to be offered steak and chips every déjeuner, every diner, every day.

Steak and chips is not a cheap meal, but it has one great advantage. It takes little time to prepare. The patronne nowadays is busy, hard-pressed. She probably has little or no help in the kitchen, she has television to watch, she has the new need to keep her children's clothes not white but whiter than white. Small wonder if she now has no time to prepare those modest but time-consuming dishes which were such a basic part of French cooking. Gone are the untinned soups, blanquette de veau, boeuf bourguignon, tripe à la mode de Caen, pot au feu, anything requiring a sauce. You are left with fried steak; not the thick rich steaks, not the Châteaubriants, but the thin entrecôte, the grey bifteck. Or sometimes, by way of a change, fried escalope of veal and chips. There was a time, I believe, when the French had all sorts of ideas for dealing with potatoes – sauté, rissolé, en cocotte and many more. But now even the humble boiled potato is hard to find; for the British are not the only race who wish to eat chips with everything.

To compensate for the monotony, you will be given a hard stream of propaganda: here we prefer to eat very well, our entrecôte pommes frites is very much recommended, with a good dinner one must drink a good wine. And to be fair to Madame, she is giving the French what they seem to enjoy most. To many Frenchmen the only thing wrong with steak and chips is the price. One man told me frankly that he would gladly eat it every day for the rest of his life if he could afford it. Madame is being quite sincere when she tells you how good her food is; when she points out that with a good entrecôte one must have a good wine, perhaps a bottle of good Beaujolais. But I for one could not help looking back nostalgically to Burgundy, or forward hopefully to Paris where they sometimes see things differently.

The point about the two worlds, the two cultures, was made again for me the next day in Fontainebleau. I had been round the palace, I had been round the beautiful gardens. It was a glorious day and everything glowed with October sunlight. The Porte

Dorée, where the ladies saw the gentlemen off to their hunting, was gilded indeed. Only poor pious Madame de Maintenon's apartments were cut off from the sunlight, and, for that matter, from all daylight and fresh air. I had seen Napoleon's camp bed, his beautiful escritoire, his first (1814) instrument of abdication. I had stood at the exact point on the right-hand branch of the great double staircase in the Cour des Adieux, the point where, a year before Waterloo, he had said a final heart-broken farewell to the Old Guard. And now I was hot, footsore and hungry.

I walked along the rue Denecourt in the town, looking for lunch, studying the menus posted outside all the many restaurants. The choice was simple: steak and chips among the French or haute cuisine among the Anglo-Saxons. I knew that I could not eat another entrecôte frite for at least another forty-eight hours, and so I chose haute cuisine, the big hotel, the white tablecloth, the menu gastronomique. There I ate poulet sauté Aprémont, surrounded by what seemed to be a NATO Women's Luncheon Club. Not a word of French was audible in the room.

21

It was Gibbings again who led me to Valvins, to the Hotel 'Aux Rosiers', and here at least little had changed since his day. Monsieur Martin, the proprietor, was, like Gibbings himself, now dead. But Madame Martin was still as perky as a chaffinch, smiling a welcome at me. When she saw Gibbings's book under my arm, her welcome redoubled. I could have Monsieur Gibbings's old bedroom with the view over the Seine, and his special armchair. She did an imitation of him and her husband together, leaning on the bar talking, pouring out bottles, filling their glasses, never changing their positions. Soon we were following their good example. Madame Martin caught sight of my camera case whose strap was broken. I must give it to her, she said. She would get it mended for me the next morning in Fontainebleau.

The Hotel 'Aux Rosiers' has a shaded terrasse, complete with roses, beside the Seine, and it must be a pleasant place to eat during the summer. Fine though the weather was, it was too late in the year for that now; but the hotel dining-room was agreeable enough – chintz curtains, copper saucepans on the walls, red table-cloths. The television was turned unobtrusively low and Madame Martin, though she did the cooking herself, had ideas on food which went far beyond steak and chips.

Her dining-room was usually crowded with men who were working loading and unloading the sand and gravel barges at the little quay beside the bridge. They were seasonal labour, who lived in the hotel annexe and took their meals in the hotel. This surprised me for you do not usually find British workmen wishing to eat five-course meals twice a day, nor to pay fifteen shillings a time for it. Perhaps it was simply that they, like myself, knew a good thing when they found it.

The forest of Fontainebleau comes thickly down a hillside to the edge of the Seine just opposite 'Aux Rosiers', a dense tangle of trees: oaks, ashes, beeches, sycamores, chestnuts, poplars. I had timed it perfectly. In the month I had been travelling down the river, autumn had been steadily coming on and now the forest flamed before my eyes; a wild riot of colour from beechen red to poplar yellow, reflected in the smooth barge-rippled Seine.

Valvins is a very peaceful place. Left far behind was the bustle of Montereau and Saint-Mammès. There is little traffic, little sound. The hush of the forest is upon it, far more so than round Fontainebleau itself, where the silence is all too often shattered by the bangs from the firing-range. It was pleasant to stroll in the forest, crunching the leaves underfoot, listening to the birds, hoping, or perhaps only half hoping, to meet a boar; pleasant to wander by the river, to stand on the bouncy, temporary bridge and stare down at the river and at the dinghies with their blue and white sails. The Seine is wide enough here for regattas, but on cloudless, windless autumn days, with neither breeze nor current, the boats were as motionless as everything else at Valvins. Only the barges passing up or down every minute or two were a reminder of the busy world round the bend of the river.

It was pleasant too to sit at my bedroom window or on the

terrasse and watch the colours drain from the forest in the dusk.
Best of all, perhaps, was to sit on the terrasse of 'Aux Rosiers' after
a large lunch and watch the colours and the light-blue sky and the
shimmering river and the barges moving endlessly before my
eyes, and wonder if any of them were *Sacolève*, and feel my head
nodding, the book sliding from my fingers, my eyes –

I was aware of a policeman standing beside me. I started up
guiltily, wondering what crime I had committed. It seemed that
when I had filled in the hotel fiche, bemused by the warmth of my
welcome, I had inadvertently put down the date of my last entry
into France for my date of birth.

'Just six weeks old!' The policeman beamed at me. 'What a
beautiful big baby!'

Two distinguished men are associated with the bridge at
Valvins. One was Mallarmé who lived his last years in the house
next to 'Aux Rosiers'. He liked, it is said, to smoke an evening
cigar on the bridge and contemplate the scene. The other was that
dashing American, General Patton, whose army forced the crossing here in 1944. It is difficult to imagine two more dissimilar
men, the introvert and the extrovert. But they did have one thing
in common, the ability to cloak their thoughts in a vivid and
personal language, celebrated if perhaps rather limited. I wonder,
though, what the two men would have thought of each other if
they could ever have met.

22

Samois, some two miles further downstream, is larger than
Valvins, almost a town, with steep cobbled streets winding down
the hill to the river. Here too everything was flaming with
autumn across the water, silvery ilexes silhouetted against the
blazing chestnuts and poplars. Samois has a pretty waterfront, a
meandering line of cafés, restaurants, shops; the first glassed-in
terrasses chauffées, the first signs of Parisian life, the first harbingers
of winter. Along the waterfront, sheltered from the main stream

by a narrow island, was a jostling line of rowing-boats, canoes, sailing-dinghies, motor-boats. For Samois is a sporting place. Across the river, on the weir side, was a line of fishermen, and behind them lawns, country houses, the village of Hericy.

I wandered along the front at Samois. Coming towards me were two remarkably pretty girls in Capri pants and sweaters. Before even hearing their voices I knew they were American. Behind them came two gaunt women in tweeds, towing small dogs. Before even hearing their voices I knew they were British. I was, I realized, within strolling distance of the NATO Country Club.

I walked up to the lavoir where an old woman was scrubbing some sheets. It was a beautiful lavoir, she said, so convenient. One did not need a washing-machine with a beautiful lavoir like this.

I asked if she did all her washing in cold water.

Certainly not, she said. She brought buckets of hot water from her house. It was most convenient.

There was something stunning about such indomitable cheerfulness. I expect she talked like that in February too.

Melun prides itself on being built on the same pattern as Paris: first an island in the Seine, with a large church and a château, and later everything spreading on to both banks in a tangle of avenues and small streets. However, the result is less enticing. The church has been much restored, the château replaced by flour mills, while behind the church is a large and important prison, with high walls and towers patrolled by armed warders. The Seine is lined with willows and fishermen and spanned by a graceful new bridge. But personally I like to remember Melun for something quite different – cheese. For at last I was in great cheese country.

One glance at the cheese board on my way into dinner showed the promise of what was to come. This was no moment to waste an appetite on steak and chips.

'Instead of hors d'oeuvres,' I said, 'I will have cheese.'

'Fromage, monsieur?'

'And instead of a grillade I will have more cheese.'

'Fromage, monsieur?'

'And after that cheese as usual. And a bottle of Moulin à Vent.'

There were hurried consultations at the back and finally the patron brought me the cheese board.

'Fromage à gogo,' I commented.

'There is plenty more outside, monsieur,' he said. 'Bon appetit!'

One of the greatest wine and cheese parties of all time was given at the Congress of Vienna by Talleyrand in an effort to restore French prestige. Guests were invited to choose from sixty different cheeses from many countries. The comments of the Tsar, the Duke of Wellington and Castlereagh have not been recorded, but Metternich had to admit that Brie was the greatest of them all. Personally I think that Metternich, for all his failings as a statesman, showed on this occasion good judgment.

Accordingly I only gave a passing nod to such interesting local cheeses as Ville Saint Jacques and Friandises, and concentrated on the Bries. There were four of them. Brie de Meaux, eaten in segments cut from its large disc, creamy, soft-rinded, with its subtle unforgettable taste; the cheese known all the world over simply as Brie, but which is never the same when sold in thin triangular boxes; the basic Brie, primus inter pares.

Or Brie de Montereau, cut from a much smaller disc and therefore eaten in larger slices, bigger mouthfuls. Rather drier than Brie de Meaux; was it, I wondered, even better, even subtler?

Or Brie de Coulommiers, in a smaller disc still not much bigger than a Camembert, but nearly twice as thick. Brie de Coulommiers is made from the same milk culture as the other two Bries, but its greater thickness gives it a different goût as it matures, the first taste creamier, the last perhaps earthier, farmhousier. Coulommiers is unfortunately not an appellation controlée, like the other Bries, and some very strange cheeses sometimes get sold under that name. But on this occasion it was perfect, the best of them all, my favourite.

Or Brie de Melun, smaller than a Montereau, larger than a Coulommiers. Brie de Melun is quite different from the others, a browner cheese, a browner harder rind. Its texture was more like a Pont L'Evêque, but its taste was all its own: strong, much stronger than any of the others, with a final echo – can a cheese have an echo? – of ripe blue Cheshire. With my passion for strong cheeses, I realized that Brie de Melun might have been made especially for me, my favourite. And then I started again on Brie de Meaux, the greatest of them all . . .

The French, unexpectedly, take pride in the fact that Brie is good for the health as it replaces in the intestinal tract important bacteria which might have been destroyed earlier by antibiotics. But this was not the aspect of Brie which I wanted to consider chiefly on that happy evening in Melun.

The next day, being Saturday, I went to the local market, where the whole of Melun went to shop. It was a jolly, bustling, noisy crowd, many of them unexpectedly Spanish and buying fish, particularly eels, at the really enormous fish counters. But I, like a true Ben Gunn, went to the cheese counters where I bought splendidly smelly cheeses and packed them away gaily in my suitcase among my shirts. Bries are matured by local artisans, self-employed cheese merchants, and one of them was Monsieur Guy Steinbach whom I met selling cheese at his stall. Why did I not visit him at his home that afternoon, he suggested, and he would be delighted to show me his racks of cheese.

So that afternoon I got off the bus in the village of Lieusaint, some ten miles away. Lieusaint consisted of one straight street disappearing into a remote faultless vanishing point. It was in the middle of the plain, and straight poplar-lined roads radiated from it in all directions. It had, apparently, one church, one café, two nuns, and I did not think very much of it until I reminded myself that I was really walking, squat and stubby, into a Utrillo picture.

Monsieur Steinbach took me round his immaculate cheese rooms, explaining the process. The whole thing started at the local farms or laiteries where he bought the 'raw' cheeses. It took fourteen litres of milk to make one Brie de Melun cheese. The milk itself didn't matter much; best was a mixture of Norman and Friesian cow milk, partly skimmed to prevent an ammoniac taste appearing. The culture itself was kept in the farms and laiteries, renewed every few days in fresh milk and never allowed to die. The embryonic cheeses would then be put in a metal strainer of appropriate size and left both to drain and to acquire their characteristic shape. At this stage Monsieur Steinbach would buy them, thick white discs.

He would keep them first for ten days in an upstairs room warm and well-ventilated, and allow them to dry. Then they would be transferred to a cellar, where they would be kept for two months. As I entered the cellar the smell of ammonia was overpowering. My eyes began to pour and I was irresistibly reminded of the teargas chamber on army gas courses. With annoyance I noticed that neither Monsieur Steinbach nor his two-year-old son who accompanied us reacted at all. Through my tears I looked at the rows of cheeses on their straw mats on their racks, gradually turning brown. Monsieur Steinbach would turn them over every three days and change their straw, for all the world as if they were animals – which I suppose in a sense they were.

'Isn't it warm?' he said.

I agreed. It was pretty hot in the cellar, though this was not the chief of my discomforts.

'All done by the cheeses,' he said. 'There is no other heating in here.'

I looked at the rows of Bries de Melun, blurrily, in awe.

Sadly the demand for Brie de Melun seems to be declining. I should like to eat it regularly but it is rare to find it in a restaurant or crêmerie outside Melun. It does not seem to travel well; if you put it in a box – and the merchants like their cheeses boxed – it ferments too fast and gets too hot; if you put it in a vacuum pack, the culture dies and a different, ammoniac fermentation sets in. It is also more expensive than the others, taking so much milk, so much time to mature. And finally there is the fact that a large number, I suspect an increasing number, of Frenchmen, not only in Burgundy but elsewhere, prefer their cheese immature, chalky white. 'Pas trop fait' are words I often hear while queuing in my local crêmerie in Paris for cheese. All the same, it would be nice to meet Brie de Melun from time to time elsewhere.

Brie de Melun was Monsieur Steinbach's first interest, but he matured the other Bries too. These did not need to spend a preliminary period in the drying room and were matured in a different cellar, kept much cooler (46–50 degrees Fahrenheit) with the aid of gas-refrigeration. Brie de Montereau had the smallest milk content of the four and only took ten days to mature. It was also, naturally, the cheapest. Coulommiers, being small, also took only ten days to mature. Brie de Meaux took six to eight weeks to mature, almost as long as Brie de Melun, but of course there was no preliminary drying period. Being cooler, they matured more gently, and I did not find myself called upon to weep before them too.

I did, however, find myself thinking anxiously of my suitcase in Monsieur Steinbach's hall. Apart from the chemical warfare angle, the thing must be red-hot by now.

23

Though there are fishermen in plenty on one branch of the Seine in Melun, the river there is primarily something to be used. But by the time it reaches the pretty stone village of Boissise-le-Bertrand some two miles further on, it is once again recreational; fishing, sailing, rowing, camping. A regatta was going on and a company of Girl Guides was doing mysterious things with maps. The Seine flowed peacefully through open parkland, dotted with oaks and country houses, until it reached the town of Corbeil-Essonnes.

I spent the night in Corbeil, which was, on reflection, an error. It was difficult to find a bed, since all the hotels seemed to be full with seasonal labour staying there for weeks on end. It was difficult to find anywhere to eat even à la française. The town is heavily industrialized; since the Middle Ages it has been the granary of France, and the present huge mills are the most important in France. There are also a big paper-mill, an enormous printing works and several other large factories. As I wandered about the streets at night I felt as if I were in the North of England, perhaps Wigan. And like the North of England everyone goes to bed early in Corbeil. By nine o'clock it was a deserted town.

But it woke up on Sunday morning for the market. It was a big market, both in the quantities displayed and in their variety; local produce, food, clothes. I was glad to see my friend Monsieur Steinbach selling his cheeses at a stall. The shoppers were good-natured, jolly, and most of them I noticed were men.

All this was on the left bank of the Seine. Now that it was daylight I discovered that the part of Corbeil on the right bank was quite different – something which no one had thought fit to tell me the night before. Here were the hotels and restaurants for the managerial class; here were managerial villas with terraces facing the river instead of factories; here were boats and gardens and shrubs – a Thames Valley set-up.

The two worlds were so different and yet complemented each other. On the left bank the mills and factories, the casual labourers, the market; on the right bank bowling-clubs, Rotarian lunches, chambers of commerce. And the Seine flowing thickly between them.

A few miles below Corbeil the Seine passes on its right the large forest of Sénart, which is largely used, as the French say, for equitation. Rides have been cut through the forest going right down to the water's edge and you can hire your horse by the week or the month. I was not equipped for riding, but I stayed at an attractive small hotel near Soisy; the forest was all round me, the Seine was at my feet.

The hotel had been rightly recommended to me for its food. The patronne employed a chef and I was offered home-made pâté and duck. But I was too cross to enjoy it. Never has television been more deafening, never have interviews with Olympic swimmers seemed more endlessly repetitive. I ventured to ask Madame if it could be turned down, or even off, but she said firmly that the other guests liked it. There was in fact only one other guest that night and he was reading a newspaper. Yes, he said, he was quite agreeable to the set being turned off.

The set, however, remained turned on, and Madame's eyes never left it for a second, even while she was uncorking my wine.

And the chef in the kitchen could hear it too, even though he couldn't see it just then. I sat, my back stubbornly turned to it, glaring out at the black river and mentally drafting a letter to Michelin:

Pourriez-vous indiquer dans vos guides les restaurants où la television est obligatoire pendant les repas ..

However, the next morning was golden and sunny, and my temper improved. I would walk through the forest to my next port of call, Champrosay. Madame atoned a little for those swimmers by volunteering to drive my suitcase round to Champrosay by the road. I relented sufficiently to say that I might return next year when it was possible to eat out on the terrace.

It was a very pleasant walk, first across some fields, and then through the woods along the bank of the Seine. Champrosay, I remembered, had been painted by Renoir, but I could not find his view. As I recalled it, there were hardly any trees in his picture, and I was in a dense forest.

I was early for lunch and still in a mood for exercise. I could not ride, but I could perhaps row. Could Madame la patronne lend me a boat for an hour or two? She offered me a motor-boat, but I spurned that. Something with oars, I said, gesturing suitably. She produced, rather doubtfully, a small green collapsible boat. Would that be all right, she asked? Could I swim?

I climbed in and pulled bravely out into the middle of the river. It was a very different Seine from the one I had rowed on at Marcilly. It was much wider and there was hardly any current in any direction. On the other hand, it was also much rougher, churned by the barges which went by every minute or two. In my little boat I rocked up and down like a cork in the Bay of Biscay. At one moment in the violent wash of a pousseur, my collapsible boat started to collapse. While I fought with the ribs, I saw out of the corner of my eye, another barge bearing down on me. Trying to fix the ribs with my feet, I pulled out of the way and the barge went looming by. Above me I glimpsed a familiar name. *Sacolève.*

I shouted, Monsieur Lenoir looked out and immediately

stopped the engine. Michèle and Lydie waved, Madame came on
deck to see what was going on. Our respective craft drifted apart
as we shrieked our greetings at each other. How was he, how was
I, how was Madame? Comme toujours. Had I seen any more
pousseurs, I'd send him some photographs to Montereau, what
was his address again, where was he going this trip? Au revoir,
à bientot.

I pulled back to the landing-stage. Madame had come out to see
what all the noise was about. Was I drowning, perhaps? Seeing
me shrieking goodbye to the Lenoirs, she said in a puzzled voice,
'You have friends on that barge, then?'

'Cousins,' I answered.

She looked at me in a baffled way.

Two hours later I was lying on the river bank, staring at the
black and silver river. My feet were jammed against a tree, my
head on a root. I was feeling very content. I had walked, I had
rowed, I had seen the Lenoirs again; I was full of escalope à la
milanaise; I had headed Madame la patronne off from giving me
steak and chips for lunch – quelque chose un peu spécial, as she had
called it; I had persuaded her to turn off the television. I was full of
chianti; the afternoon sun flared off the river into my eyes,
hypnotizing me.

Only one thing kept me awake. The name Champrosay was
bothering me. I had heard it before, in some other connection.
Not the Renoir picture, something else, on the tip of my memory.
Later, suddenly, a name came to me: Thibault de Champrosay.
That was the man. But who was he, what was he doing here? He
sounded like a Crusader, someone out of Zoé Oldenbourg. 'When
Count Thibault de Champrosay saw that the child was saracen-
dark, he rose wrathfully in his stirrups and beheaded the fair
Alexandrette with one stroke of his sword.' Something like
that.

I dozed off. When I woke, I remembered. Thibault de Champrosay was the name on the bottom of many of the posters
advertising exhibitions, which you see on the walls of the Flore
or the Coupole. He was the man who printed them. Not a
Crusader after all but a printer. No doubt those were his printing

works across the river. Ah well! Not so romantic perhaps, but better for poor Alexandrette.

Beyond the forest of Sénart, the farms get smaller, the building lots more frequent. Factory chimneys begin to sprout. At Villeneuve-Saint-Georges you are in the Paris conurbation. Jets roar overhead on their way into Orly. The skyline is a tangle of cranes and chimneys against the sunset, amongst them the Eiffel Tower. At Alfortville, in a landscape of factories and bridges, the Seine is joined by one of its greatest tributaries, the Marne. At Charenton it enters Paris.

Part Two: The Seine in Paris

1

The seven miles of the Seine in Paris are without doubt the most famous river-front in the world. Just as the Seine originally created Paris, so the Parisians have cherished the Seine, turning it into an attenuated water-park. It has not been allowed to become, like London's river, a straggling line of factories and wharves and cranes; or like New York's river, a spiky tangle of docksides. Paris is still a busy port. But the Seine seems to have been planned more for pleasure, for strolling, cruising, fishing, loving, boating, reading, living, sunning, sprawling, drinking, swimming, eating. The Seine is designed as something to be lived beside, to be looked at and, above all, to be enjoyed.

Despite the growth of the capital, the Seine remains the heart of Paris, or, rather, the great artery that feeds everything else. It is hardly possible to move about the centre of Paris without travelling along or across the river at some point. The streets of Paris are numbered from the end nearest the river. In the middle of the Seine, in the middle of the Île de la Cité, in front of the cathedral of Notre Dame is a brass star like a compass; Kilometre Zero, the centre of the centre of the centre of the city, the point from which all distances in France are measured.

From the river, Paris seems in summer to be a double line of trees, poplars below, planes above; and above the trees a line of famous façades interleaved with more picturesque and more irregular blocks. It has been said that to walk along the Seine is to see everything worth seeing in Paris, to learn everything worth knowing in French history. An exaggeration, of course, but, on a spring evening, an excusable one.

The Seine's entry into Paris is, however, unprepossessing. It takes four bridges to shake off the industrialism of the suburbs. The first good viewpoint is the middle of the Pont d'Austerlitz, facing downstream, and even here the eyes need to be blinkered.

Behind is a not unattractive suspension bridge carrying the métro, and on either side the two great railway stations of Lyon and Austerlitz. In front, on either bank, are two large white modern buildings of remarkable unshapeliness. Beyond the one on the left, another new building, containing new lecture rooms for the over-crowded Sorbonne, is rising on the site of the old Halle aux Vins, the wine market. A still unextinguished hope remains that this one at least will have a more suitable appearance, a more interesting skyline. On either side of the river are lines of moored barges, particularly on the right bank, on the Quai Henri IV, where there is a veritable port, another Saint-Mammès. Here too is a house-boat, the headquarters of the river police, though they are less con-cerned with the industrious, houseproud, family-loving bargees, who sometimes picnic on the quay, than with suicides, collisions and the dumping of refuse. But the great view is dead down-stream: the wide river curving away, the old houses of the Île Saint-Louis, the fuzz of trees, and on the skyline the towers of Notre Dame.

The quais of the Seine, as almost all the world knows, are double-decker affairs. The upper deck contains the road along which a deafening torrent of one-way traffic pours, occasionally held palpitating at bay for a few tentative seconds by a red light or a policeman. Between the road and the river is a wide pavement with pedestrians and heavily pollarded planes: the inhabitants walking determinedly to the nearest bus stop, the tourists pausing to consult their maps or look at the view or lean over the edge. Here too, on top of the parapet, are the green bookstalls, their wares haphazardly dripping down the walls like bright waterfalls. They are carefully licensed, traditional affairs; but nowadays their prints seem usually to be reproductions of Bernard Buffet, their books, with the change of policy about obscenity in Britain and America, more often Sartre than Henry Miller; and the green boxes themselves are being replaced by larger aluminium ones.

The lower deck is beside the water and reached by occasional steps from the upper level, or by boat. It is an informal cobbled way, shaded by great trees, interrupted by small gardens, or, more regrettably, by car-parks or chutes for loading rubble into barges, or by the abrupt end of the quay, for this lower deck is not continuous. Here we find the fishermen, those patient indefatigable men who spend so much time with so little reward. It is not true that no one has ever seen a fish caught, but it is surprising that the tiny fish should be worth not only taking but keeping. However, fishing, as has often been explained to me, is less a question of catching fish than an excuse to dawdle in idyllic surroundings, and the fishermen of Paris have this in abundance.

Here too we find the loving couples hand in hand, or breaking all records in the endurance of their kissing; young solitary girls sitting on newspapers, dangling their legs over the edge, reading Bergson if they are very young, or *Paris-Dimanche* if they are older; clochards lying down like thick bundles of overcoats tied up in string; bargees setting a reluctant foot on dry land. Where these lower quays meet the bridges, they pass under arches and here, sous les ponts de Paris, the lovers find greater privacy and the clochards shelter from the rain.

This is the Seine of legend and nostalgia, the imperishable romance which is about to perish for ever. The fishermen, the lovers, the clochards, the girls reading Bergson, the strollers, many of the trees, most of the barges, are to be swept away by the barbarous new express motorways along the verges of the Seine. The project, which is already under construction, will allow another hundred thousand vehicles a day, on each bank, to cross the middle of Paris, with all their noise and fumes.

The express motorways, it is proudly announced, are to be non-stop routes from one side of Paris to the other, and there would seem to be no good reason why such traffic could not be channelled round the outskirts of the city on a ring road – except that such a road would be a slightly longer route. One of the sad things about the French is the way it is taken for granted by everyone that the demands of traffic must take automatic priority over all other human needs. When I commented to a Frenchman that it was hardly possible to walk along the street now with all the cars parked on the pavements, he answered without sympathy, 'Mais naturellement, the cars have to find parking somewhere' – as if they were humans too, or gods. It is significant that the project for the Seine motorways, which will destroy the beauty and the peace of that lovely river-front for ever, has aroused no whisper of protest from any person, organization or newspaper.

The quais which alone will remain undamaged are, of course, those on the two islands: the larger Île de la Cité, the original Paris, and the smaller Île Saint-Louis in its wake, like a dinghy towed behind a galleon. There is already a lot of cross-island, cross-river traffic, but short of building an autoroute along the middle of the river, or clearing both islands and turning them both into car-parks, it would seem that these at least are safe from those cold traffic planners who would like to turn Paris into another Los Angeles. Here will still be, I hope, the two quiet islands, the still centre of the storm, the last refuge of the fishermen and the clochards and the lovers. Even now, walking along the quays of the Île Saint-Louis, it is possible to recapture the feeling of what the quais of the Seine meant to earlier generations, before the war, before the car explosion. This is perhaps why there so often seems to be a film being shot on location on one or other of the Île Saint-Louis quais. A night stroller may find bodies being humped into motor-boats, or clochards shrugging humorously, or Jean Gabin contemplating suicide under the glare of arc-lights, surrounded by clouds of script-girls.

The quickest and least satisfying method of seeing the Seine is by car (or, of course, by métro). The most expensive is by bâteau-mouche, those extraordinary craft that look like huge insects with big eyes. On a summer's day you can sit on deck and admire the passing panorama; at Easter it is usually much chillier. Or you can go romantically by night, eating a sophisticated candlelit dinner and peering out through the condensation on the windows. Every lover of the Paris Seine should make the daylight trip at least once. The snag is that it is all over so quickly, that you are swept past places where you might like to linger, that you are cut off from the shore. For this reason the best, and cheapest, way of seeing the Seine is on foot; and because of the traffic on the mainland quays, it is best to stay on the islands as long as possible.

2

The stern of the Île Saint-Louis is a gravelly garden full of scream-
ing children clambering over benches. The point of the island on
the lower waterside level – the rudder, so to speak, of the island – is
a paved sunny triangle with wide horizons. Passing by on a
bâteau-mouche some eight years ago I had expressed a sudden and
unforeseen wish to sunbathe on that point. But there was not the
opportunity for it on that particular holiday in Paris. However, a
year later I made the hero of a novel I was writing sunbathe there,
in the same spirit that palaeolithic man drew pictures of the beasts
he hoped to catch later. When I finally came to live about two
hundred yards away, I was able to make my wish come true as
and when I wanted.

I chose a hot Whitsun. I went down to the point, spread out a
newspaper, took off my shirt, lay down and closed my eyes.
Others were doing it too and it was as enjoyable as my hero had
found it five years before – except for one detail. What I had as a
novelist failed to imagine was that the air about four foot above
my face would whirr continuously with the whip of fishing lines
cast by inexpert fishermen under instruction from the local fishing
school. It prevented total relaxation.

The Île Saint-Louis was originally two islands: the Île Notre
Dame downstream was the larger; the upstream island was called
the Île des Vaches, from the cows which were brought there to
graze. Both islands, which were flooded when the Seine was high,
were uninhabited, and the property of the monks of Notre Dame.
King Philippe Auguste built a tower on the Île Notre Dame in the
twelfth century for the defence of the City, and later Saint Louis
built a small oratory there for the occasions when he came to the
island. The monks organized occasional fairs there, and it was a
popular place for duels.

It was Henri IV who first approved a plan for embanking the
islands and building on them, but work did not begin till the reign

of his son, Louis XIII. The monks disposed of their rights, to their later great regret, to a contractor called Marie (after whom the bridge is named). Marie made a fortune out of reselling the land to those who rushed to build themselves handsome new town houses. These were not the established nobility, who already had hotels of their own, but ambitious bourgeois on the make: bankers, contractors, merchants; or those who had found their fortunes in the Royal Chamber or the Royal Accounts; the ancestors, in either case, of a new generation of aristocrats.

They were a motley collection and social life on the Île must have been difficult. On one quay alone, the new proprietors included the Corrector of Accounts in the Royal Chamber, one of the twelve hautbois players in the Royal Chamber, the Grand Master of Waters and Forests, the Queen Mother's private painter and valet, the Captain of the Queen's Regiment, an iron merchant, the Governor of the Bastille, the President of the Chamber of Accounts, a gentleman with the baffling title of Lieutenant de la Robe Longue à la Connetablie de France, and the Professor of Arabic at the Collège de France. An assembly of many talents, united by intelligence, a wish to succeed and a wish to live on the Île Saint-Louis.

But if their duties were diverse, their houses were of uniform style. The whole island was built up during the same period in the middle of the seventeenth century, a particularly good date of French architecture. Many of the houses were designed by the King's chief architect, Louis Le Vau, who built himself an attractive hotel at 3 Quai d'Anjou. From the beginning the new island was designed as an architectural whole, though without the rigid symmetry of the Place Vendôme or the Place des Vosges. The houses on the Île Saint-Louis differ from each other in size and shape, but they blend admirably in their style and proportions.

Over the centuries the Île declined in prestige. The big hotels became apartment houses for impoverished bourgeois or working class families. There was no wish to rebuild in later florid styles and almost the only nineteenth-century rebuilding is at the downstream end of the island. Now the area is once again fashionable, but much of the island is officially protected, and there is hope that it will remain, architecturally at any rate, intact, a gem of seventeenth-century grace. It can be said that there are only two really ugly buildings on the island, both from this century. A famous American novelist lives in one, I live in the other; and we console ourselves with the theory that it is better to live in an ugly house and look across at a beautiful, if rather rickety, one, than the other way round.

The plan of the island is very simple: a long central straight street, the rue Saint-Louis-en-l'Île, running the length of the island with occasional side streets branching off it at right angles. The views from the houses round the quais are wide, the views and the streets themselves inside the island are very narrow, as was usual in seventeenth-century Paris. One street, the rue de Bretonvilliers, is even spanned by a building in a graceful arch. And just as there are two views, so there are two worlds on the island. On the outside quais are the large luxurious flats of the rich, the titled, the diplomats, the film-stars, the world of Tout-Paris, as it is called. Inside the island, in the rue Saint-Louis-en-l'Île and its side streets, the island's intestine, as Aragon so charmingly put it, everything is humbler. Here are the small shops, cafés, modest hotels, tradesmen. Here are the true islanders.

They have lived all their life on the island, like their fathers and grandfathers before them. Many of them seem to be only about four foot high, and they often have medieval names like Basseporte or Crèvecoeur. They go as rarely as possible to the mainland and it is said that some have never been off the island, though it is hard to credit this. Certainly one old man told me he had not been on the mainland for over forty years. It is a world of its own and though many tourists visit the island they sometimes feel it to be forbidding and exclusive. Balzac complained that the place made him nervous. But once inside, once admitted as an islander, everything is cosy and friendly. We mind each other's business, gossip and joke while queueing in the shops, exchange news, take an interest in future plans and projects. The Île Saint-Louis is still a country village, cut off from the rest of the city by the big houses on the quais and by the Seine.

Tout-Paris, however, is encroaching all the time, as the area becomes more valuable. More and more small shops – cobblers, grocers, pâtisseries – are finding it pays them to sell out, take their profit and move to the suburbs or the country. Bookshops which sell only books and the small dark-brown bars which provide not only vins but also bois, charbons, liqueurs et billards seem to be especially vulnerable. In their place are coming antique shops and intimate, rather expensive, candlelit restaurants. Despite the lack of parking facilities, the island is slowly becoming a place where the well-to-do from the sixteenth arrondissement come to spend an amusing evening.

However, for all this, the Île Saint-Louis is still a charming place to live, a quiet area for a stroll, a good viewpoint for the river. If, like most islanders, you walk down the rue Saint-Louis-en-l'Île, you will only see the Seine at the end of each cross street. But you will see many other things of interest: for instance the amazing moment at half-past eleven and half-past five every day when the street is suddenly flooded with children, for there are many schools on the island. One of them is housed in the building which spans the rue de Bretonvilliers; between lessons the girls, one of them my daughter, peer out of their windows at me, giggling; and across the street, a few yards of air away, I wave back over my typewriter.

Further up the street, beyond the rue Poulletier, the ancient divide between the two islands, you will find the shops: the butcher and the dry-cleaner who take such an interest in modern art; the wine-merchant who gives such astute advice ('If your guests are French, they will prefer whisky to champagne'); the crêmerie ('Monsieur, I shall refuse to sell you my cheeses if you will persist in drinking lemonade with them' – said, I hasten to say, not to me but to a Frenchman who was also in the shop); the electrician with his enormous collection of monumental puns; the greengrocer who had been stunned to learn that my wife had served in an anti-aircraft battery during the last war, and now addresses her politely as 'Mon Capitaine' (not 'Ma Capitaine').

Here also is the island church, Saint-Louis en l'Île. It is a popular church for weddings. I recall two during my first week on the island. One was a big affair. The bride was a rich girl from the

1 The Seine channelled through the temple of Sequana, the goddess of the river

2 The original Sequana found buried on the site

3 The grotto of the City of Paris built over the principal source of the Seine, complete with a nineteenth-century Sequana

4 *Left* The first bridge over the Seine

5 *Below* The church and the island at Châtillon-sur-Seine

6 *Above* The source of the Douix, the Seine's most spectacular tributary

7 *Right* The gigantic
vase of Vix, dating
from the sixth
century BC

8 A typical old street with half-timbered houses in Troyes

9 Monsieur and Madame Lenoir and Lydie on their highly polished barge, *Sacolève*

10 'Brie de Melun'

11 *Above* The Paris islands. The Île de la Cité with Notre Dame and behind it the Île Saint-Louis

12 *Opposite* The bow windows of the seventeenth-century Hotel Lambert overlooking the Seine

13 The tourist's memory of Paris: bookstalls and gendarmes

14 The Pont Marie and the Île Saint-Louis

15 Under the bridges of Paris: Notre Dame and the Quai d'Orléans seen from a barge below the Pont de la Tournelle

16 The Île de la Cité painted by Corot in 1833, before Haussmann swept away the old buildings

17 The Pont Neuf and some of the remaining old houses on the Île de la Cité

18 *Above* The grace of the seventeenth-century Pont Royal contrasts with the ponderous Louvre

19 *Opposite above* The most flamboyant of all the Seine bridges: the Pont Alexandre III in 1900, the year of its completion

20 *Opposite below* The statue of Liberty, a return gift from the American people, stands on an island at the entrance of Paris

21 The poet Stéphane Mallarmé as portrayed by Manet

22 Claude Monet at work at Argenteuil, painted by Manet

23 A portrait of Sisley by Renoir

24 Houseboats on the Seine near Paris

25 The white cliffs of Les Andelys

26 *Above* Near the Côte des Deux Amants. The Amfreville locks and the Poses Dam can be seen in the background

27-9 *Opposite* 'The Romantic Seine' (*Top*) La Roche Guyon and its château built into the rock. (*Centre*) Les Andelys and the ruins of Château Gaillard. (*Below*) La Bouille at the foot of Robert le Diable's castle

30 Total Rouen: hills, towers and cranes

31 Rouen's island and quays: a startling contrast with the Seine in Paris

32 The abbey at Jumièges, the Seine's loveliest ruin

33 (*Right*) At Villequier: changing the pilot

34 (*Below*) The Tancarville suspension bridge, built in 1959, the last bridge across the Seine

35 The end of the river: Le Havre

Quai d'Orléans. She wore an haute couture dress, and drove away afterwards in a Cadillac, waving, at least as far as the traffic jam further down the street. The other bride was a true islander, a very small girl, and her wedding was very small too. She did not even have a small car to take her away from the church. Instead she walked, with the wedding party. As I was going in the same direction, I joined them, and we marched along, singing and waving, the bride still in her home-made dress. At the end of the street we turned left over the Pont Sully, down the steps into Métro Sully-Morland. There we parted, she to Direction Ivry and a wedding breakfast at her uncle's, I to Direction Saint-Gervais.

Weddings apart, the church is of considerable interest. It is of the same date as the rest of the island, though it took rather longer to build. The spire – one of the few remaining spires in Paris – is pierced with a pattern of ovals, which seen from below gives a curious asymmetrical effect. The clock, which loudly strikes the half-hours, hangs out over the street and the main door is a finely carved affair of wood, encrusted with cherubs and garlands of leaves and acorns, worthy of the contemporary Grinling Gibbons himself.

Further up the street is another elaborate doorway, its portal supported by two large stone gryphons and one sea-god. Here, in the Hotel Chenizot (and not in Number 13, as is sometimes said), Thérèsia Cabarrus honeymooned with her first husband, the Chevalier de Fontenay. Both were rich and the marriage was arranged by their parents, who saw a good chance of uniting the two fortunes. They were an ill-matched pair; Thérèsia was partly Spanish, proud, tall, beautiful, already voluptuous although she was only fourteen; the curves of her bust and thighs, which were later to become so famous, were already showing. Her husband, on the contrary, was small, red-faced and ugly, and Thérèsia was ashamed to be seen with him. Apart from their money they had nothing in common. Fontenay's chief interest was in raising himself in the nobility. His title of Chevalier was self-awarded, but in 1789, a month after the fall of the Bastille, a time when aristocrats of longer lineage were beginning to think about packing their trunks, he succeeded in buying a genuine marquisate. His young marquise was more interested in revolutionary politics. Her drawing-room on the Île Saint-Louis was full of the more progressive nobility like Lafayette and the brothers La Rochefoucauld. Thérèsia herself joined the Club des Feuillants and generally, it is said, played with the Revolution like a child.

However, eventually the Fontenays had to flee Paris; the marquis to America, Thérèsia to Bordeaux, in theory to her parents, in practice to a dungeon, to the bed of Citizen Tallien, the ferocious dictator of Bordeaux, and in due course to her historic role as the sex-symbol of the Revolution, Notre Dame de Thermidor. There is no record that she revisited the Île Saint-Louis during her years of glory. She was too busy making public appearances, dressed as Liberty or Calypso or just vaguely in gold and ostrich feathers. She was fully occupied too in bearing children. She had eleven altogether by various fathers; as Napoleon said, 'She has the bastards of the whole world', including, possibly, himself. Her eldest child, however, Antoine de Fontenay, was born on the Île Saint-Louis a year after her first marriage. And in 1815 she made a last return to the island to see Antoine die of wounds received in the war.

Thirty-three years later, in the same Hotel Chenizot, the Archbishop of Paris also died of wounds, received at the barricades in the Faubourg Saint-Antoine. The story shows that he was not a true islander, for the Louisiens have always held themselves aloof from the riots and street-fighting in the other parts of Paris. Only twice have they risen in revolt: once was in 1844 to protest (successfully) against having to pay tolls to cross to the mainland; the second time, a hundred years later, to throw out the Germans, a feat which they achieved, to their pride, several days before the next door Île de la Cité.

Wanderers more interested in the Seine than the island itself would, however, do better to stay on one of its two banks. The northern bank consists of the Quai d'Anjou and the Quai de Bourbon. The first house, on the corner of the Quai and the rue Saint-Louis-en-l'Île, is the Hotel Lambert, the grandest house on the island. It was built by Le Vau for Lambert le riche, who had studied the art of embezzlement under Louis XIII's superintendent

of finances, Claude de Bullion. Here Rousseau had an affair with
Madame Dupin, Voltaire with Madame du Châtelet. In 1830 the
Hotel was acquired by Prince Czartoryski and became the centre
of Polish life in Paris. Chopin was often there, and one Polish
writer remarked to me that 'we Poles think of it as the British
think of Windsor Castle'. During the last war it was the secret
hiding-place of allied airmen shot down over France. Passed down
the pipeline, they would end up in the Hotel Lambert to be given
civilian clothes and forged papers. Then they would be allowed
out to sight-see, provided that they promised not to utter a word.
When the Germans searched the house, the concierge would give
a special ring on the bell, and the airmen would lose themselves
in the complicated cellars until the danger was over.

The Hotel Lambert is a fine building, with bow windows, long
galleries and wide views. The curtains of the galleries never seem
to be drawn, and on winter evenings, crossing the Pont Sully, you
look in at glittering chandeliers, gold-tooled books, painted ceil-
ings showing the labours of Hercules, a peep into a past century.
The garden seen from the upper rooms is a sad flowerless desert of
gravel and trees. But from the street, over the wall, it is a summer
hedge of lilac, chestnut candle and lime blossom, twittering with
song birds. The imposing courtyard has a double staircase of stone,
decorated with a fresco by Le Sueur showing the Seine as a shaggy
old man being rejuvenated by the Île Saint-Louis in the person of
a fierce, bare-bosomed young woman – not, one must feel, a con-
ception which would have appealed either to Saint-Louis or to
Sequana.

A few yards down the Quai d'Anjou is the famous Hotel de
Lauzun. Like the Hotel Lambert it is built with the principal
rooms on the first and second floors, to avoid flooding. It has a
river-level entrance to the kitchens, through which the son of
Monsieur de Pimodan, the aristocratic owner, was able to make
his escape during the Terror, while his father was arrested upstairs. The façade was intended to be more ornate, but the contractor was arrested for selling non-existent fuel to the army,
before the work was complete. The first floor rooms are decorated
in a fairly plain Louis XIII style, but upstairs it is a riot of Louis XIV

baroque. Every available square centimetre of surface is covered with clouds, rivers, swathes, trumpets, goddesses and masks.

The Hotel is largely known as being the scene of Lauzun's short stormy married life with La Grande Mademoiselle. The story has been often retold in romances and the characters are familiar: Lauzun, the penniless adventurer, the quarrelsome duelling bantam, the conqueror of women, the touchy braggart, the King's favourite, the Captain of the Musketeers; and La Grande Mademoiselle, the King's niece, the richest and most eligible heiress in Europe, high, wide and far from handsome, whom nobody would marry though Richelieu and Mazarin in turn had tried to match her with the King of Spain, the future Charles II of England, the Holy Roman Emperor, the Archduke of the Netherlands, and even her cousin Louis XIV. Most unwisely, she had taken part in the Fronde rising against the king, leading the assault up the scaling ladders at Orléans and for a time driving Mazarin from power. At the age of forty-two, a large ugly obscure spinster, she fell hopelessly for the little upstart.

How Lauzun's heart must have sunk when she first smiled on him. She pinned him down despite his evasions, obtained permission, almost immediately withdrawn, to marry him, secretly married him, and saw him taken at once by his brother musketeer d'Artagnan to long imprisonment on royal orders. Mademoiselle, in justice, did her best to get him out. She begged, petitioned, intrigued, bribed and poured out much of her fortune and estates; and it is typical of her ineptitude that she should have bribed the waning royal mistress, Madame de Montespan, who no longer had the influence to do all she promised. However, he was finally released after ten years and four months of captivity and the couple were reunited in March 1682 in Madame de Montespan's apartments at Saint-Germain: Lauzun, appalled at the sight of the elderly lovesick amazon he was married to, but concealing it manfully, doing his best to keep the conversation going, thanking Mademoiselle politely for her efforts on his behalf; and Mademoiselle herself, too moved to say one word.

After that, the story goes, they settled in to bourgeois married life on the Île Saint-Louis, Lauzun determined to get his own back

on the woman who had cost him his position at court, his career
and his liberty. 'Granddaughter of Henri IV,' he would say, 'take
off my boots.' The Quai d'Anjou would rock to the sound of
their quarrels and even noisier reconciliations, until after two years
she threw him out. This is the popular version, which is told today
by the official guide. Another version is that, as the marriage was
still secret, Mademoiselle could only visit him secretly. She would
come, masked, in a gondola by river, and chase him round the
house, while he escaped down a secret staircase to younger,
humbler embraces. But in fact there is no reason to think that
Mademoiselle ever set foot in the place. She was always very
royal, very conscious of etiquette. She did not come to visit
Lauzun. She summoned him to visit her.

At the start it does not seem that Lauzun set out to humiliate
his wife. Indeed, he hoped to move in with her, either at the
Luxembourg or at her château at Choisy, just outside Paris. But
Mademoiselle would not permit this. He was to lodge with
Rollinde, the intendant of her household, and visit her twice a
day, a short visit in the morning, a longer visit in the evening to
play games. Only at her château at Eu in Normandy was he
allowed to stay under the same roof, and it is far from clear that
he was allowed access to her bedroom.

It does not seem to have dawned on Mademoiselle that this
arrangement was unlikely to satisfy Lauzun for long; or if it did,
she did not care. She was, however, furious when in August 1682,
tiring of lodging with Rollinde, he bought the house on the Quai
d'Anjou. It was no part of her plan that he should own property
in Paris, and she was in no doubt of what would go on in the new
establishment. And indeed much did go on there; not only affairs
and seductions – his mistress was at the time Madeleine Fouquet –
but also gambling parties at which his guests included such
socially different persons as the Duc d'Orléans and the butcher
Tiber. Large sums changed hands, all of which was reported back
by spies to Mademoiselle, who duly reproached him on his daily
visits to her.

Lauzun's over-riding ambition was to be received at court once
more; he even underwent an improbable spiritual retreat in order

to impress Madame de Maintenon. He continually urged his wife
to plead for him but, though she had little influence herself by
now with Louis xiv, it does not seem that she even tried. She had
no great wish to see him back at court, and the present arrangements were her choice, excepting of course his infidelities. She did,
however, complain a great deal that his character was not all she
had supposed. When she fished for compliments, he did not
always respond. He told her the ribbons she wore were too young
for her, he reproached her for extravagance in redecorating
Choisy. When he was at Eu, he spent too much time out hunting,
and his quarry was not always four-legged. As a punishment for
this he was made to crawl the length of the gallery on his knees
before she would forgive him. He took of course his revenge. The
story about the hunting-boots may be apocryphal, but it seems
clear that he beat her bel et bien.

The end came the following April, 1684, at the Luxembourg.
Lauzun was hoping against hope that Louis xiv would take him to
the wars as an aide-de-camp. When this did not materialize,
Mademoiselle ordered him to leave Paris as he would look
ridiculous hanging about the capital; everyone would say it was
her fault and this would make her very angry. 'I will go away,'
answered Lauzun, 'and I will say goodbye so as never to see you
again in my life.' He bowed deeply and left.

Thereafter he prospered. He sold his house on the Quai d'Anjou
the following year and in 1688 he regained royal favour by
rescuing James ii's wife, Mary of Modena, from Whitehall; he
found, as Madame de Sevigné put it, that the road to Versailles led
through London. He commanded the French troops at the battle
of the Boyne and was made a duke by Louis xiv. At the age of
sixty-three he acquired at last a young bride, a rich heiress of fourteen, and he lived to the age of ninety. When Mademoiselle died
in 1693, he wore deep mourning, more one must think out of
panache than grief.

It was not until 1850 that the house was named after him. The
then owner, Baron Pichon, put up a large sign which is still there,
Hotel de Lausun 1657, thus getting both Lauzun's name and date
wrong. It was previously known as the Hotel de Pimodan during

the time when its most distinguished occupant lived there. Baudelaire took a lodging in the house in 1843, a humble room up the back stairs, under the roof. His friends in the Latin Quarter were amazed when he went off to live in an area which to them was outer darkness.

It was the river that drew Baudelaire. Water without limit was like genius without form, a lost sea of madness. But the Seine flowing quietly and generously between its fixed banks represented inspiration held between bounds, genius disciplined, the order in his life and work which he sought in vain to find. He spent much time looking at the Seine, and one day he saw bathing there, dressed only in her shift, his black Venus, the beautiful mulatto girl, Jeanne Duval.

Her origins are mysterious. Nor is there any contemporary agreement about her appearance. Banville described her as black, tall, crinkly haired, beautiful, with the presence of a queen, a farouche grace and something both divine and bestial. Prarond described her as not very dark, tall, crinkly haired, flat chested, walking badly. Nadar described her exuberantly large breasts, her slim hips and her graceful undulating walk. Baudelaire saw her in more poetic terms. He installed her round the corner at 6 rue Le Regrattier and she became for him the symbol of carnal, profane love; symbols were important to him.

The two years which he spent in the Hotel de Pimodan were the happiest and most ordered in Baudelaire's life; they were the longest period he ever spent in one lodging. He wrote sonnets and art criticism, he was passionately in love with Jeanne. But the shadows of disorder were closing in: lack of recognition, debt, despair. It became harder to define the poetic mists that wafted through his head. He took to spending more and more time in the Latin Quarter, less and less time either writing poetry in the Hotel de Pimodan or with Jeanne. On 30 June 1845, a time of year when the island is at its loveliest, he wrote, 'I kill myself because I am useless to others and dangerous to myself. I kill myself because I believe myself immortal and because I hope.'

He stabbed himself in a cabaret in the rue de Richelieu, in Jeanne's presence. It was an ineffective chest wound and he recovered after a few days in hospital. But he could not go back to live in the Hotel de Pimodan where his creditors had mounted guard. The idyll was over. It was something he looked back to with nostalgia. When he wrote in *L'Invitation au Voyage*

> *Là, tout n'est qu'ordre et beauté,*
> *Luxe calme et volupté,*

he was thinking not only of Jeanne's dark skin, but of the peaceful banks of the Seine.

Baudelaire did, of course, return in the following years to the Île Saint-Louis, to visit the Hotel de Pimodan and see his old friends. And it was here that he met Madame Sabatier, well known in the literary world of the Second Empire under the nickname given her by Gautier of 'La Présidente'. Aglae-Apollonie Sabatier (the 'madame' was honorary) was a jolly, pretty girl of twenty-four, chestnut-haired, friendly, self-confident. In Baudelaire's sentimental symbolism, she became his guardian angel, pure goddess, the embodiment of sacred love as contrasted with his profane love for the carnal, impure, dusky Jeanne – not that there was anything particularly sacred about Baudelaire's passion for Aglae Sabatier, and she inspired him to some terrible verse.

It was on the same occasion that he first met Gautier who was to write the famous preface to *Fleurs du Mal*. Indeed, the house was now a regular meeting place for writers and painters, drawn partly by the conversation and partly by the temptations of hashish – le club des haschichins Gautier termed their gatherings. Just who smoked and who merely watched is a matter for guesswork. Gautier presumably took hashish as he wrote a high-flown literary piece about an evening at the club and the hallucinations, the feelings of great happiness, the floating sensations attributable to hashish. Boissard, the doyen of the establishment, introduced the cult. Daumier, who lived further along the Quai, caricatured the smokers. Balzac inspected the spoonful of yellow-green paste which gave out such a strong smell of rancid butter, and declined. After all the coffee and alcohol he had absorbed, he explained, he was immune to such stuff. But the others who came to the house,

Delacroix, the Goncourt brothers, Meissonier, Steinheil, Baudelaire himself – we can only guess which were the addicts, which
tried it and abandoned it, and which abstained.

But it is certain that a great deal of hashish was smoked, judging
by the filthy state of the walls when they had done. The small
room at the eastern end of the house was particularly suitable as a
thick fug of fumes could be worked up there quite easily. When
the room was finally cleaned in 1906, a black control patch was
left in the corner for us to see, as a witness to their murky evenings
and an indication of the sad state of the haschichins' respiratory
organs.

The Hotel de Lauzun was bought by the city of Paris in 1928
and it has since been used for official receptions to visiting personages. The most famous party of recent years given there was for
the Queen and the Duke of Edinburgh on their state visit to Paris
in 1957. Musicians in eighteenth-century clothes played in the
gallery and below powdered flunkeys waited on the glittering
guests.

From the Quai d'Anjou, the most conspicuous and the most
attractive, rivermark is the Pont Marie. It was built by the original
developer of the island and the first stone was laid by Louis XIII
in 1614. On either side of the roadway was a row of small four-
storey houses and shops and these can clearly be seen in old prints
of the bridge. In 1658 severe floods destroyed the two arches
nearest to the island, together with twenty-two of the houses, and
over a hundred of the bridge's inhabitants were drowned. The
arches were rebuilt without the houses, which explains the curious
lop-sided look of the bridge in later prints. During the floods of
1740 the inhabitants were evacuated, never to return, and later the
remaining bridge-houses were pulled down. The bridge that
remains is graceful, its stone golden and mellow, and the effect is
particularly pleasing on floodlit nights.

On the corner beside the bridge is Franc Pinot's cabaret, an
ancient establishment indeed. The daughter of an earlier cabaretier
there was guillotined for trying to assassinate Robespierre. A few
yards downstream is the point where I saw my only Paris suicide.
A young man in a tartan shirt plunged into the Seine from the

right bank, facing me, forgetting in his misery that he knew how to swim. Once in the water instinct took over, and he swam slowly across the placid, half-width river and clambered out on the Île Saint-Louis, sobbing. There he hugged a poplar, watering it with tears and river-water, refusing to speak, till a klaxoned police van arrived and took him away – for it is forbidden to bathe in the Seine. What caused his despair, whether it was love, debt or failed exams, we never discovered. But, knowing Parisian youth, I would put my money on the last one.

This part of the island is called the Quai de Bourbon and it is the most peaceful part of the whole quiet island. The houses are on the same handsome pattern, their colour as subtle as that of the river or the Paris sky. At night this is replaced by warm electric street lighting (for sodium lighting has, like cinemas, been kept off the island). Louisiens seem to dislike drawing their curtains and shutting out their view. From the quai at night you catch glimpses of old rooms, of a bald head nodding with concentration over a writing desk and naturally you hope that it is concocting a novel, a poem, a speech on *le weltanschauung de la société contemporaine*, and not just accounts. Outside the huge poplars shiver black and silver in the floodlighting. Below on the water small leaking boats rock up and down in the wash of the bâteaux-mouches. Here on Sunday morning fishing clubs gather and the bank is lined by flickering rods.

It is worth leaving the island for a few steps and walking out on to the Pont Louis Philippe to see the view; the Quai de Bourbon behind its trees, the Pont Marie downstream, the curving river, compose into a charming scene. In other directions you can see the dome of the Panthéon, the towers of Saint-Gervais and the Tour Saint-Jacques and the Conciergerie. It is only the bridge itself that holds no possible interest.

The Quai de Bourbon continues to the point, the prow of the island. This is the quietest place of all, surrounded by acres of water and miles of sky, with only the boats and the high jets for company, and the silent kissing couples. Above is another enormous poplar and behind it two of Le Vau's finest houses rising like a golden cliff.

The third route along the Île Saint-Louis lies along the south side of the island, the Quai de Béthune and the Quai d'Orléans. This is the fashionable side, the sunny side; the views are wider, the left bank houses across the river more picturesque than their counterparts on the right bank. The flats here are more desirable and there has been more rebuilding. The Hotel de Bretonvilliers has disappeared, but the name, that of yet another nouveau riche contractor, lives on in the side street, the rue de Bretonvilliers. A Madame de Bretonvilliers, it is said, was the mistress of the Archbishop of Paris. Her husband, for some reason, objected to this; when the archbishop tried to slip away discreetly, Monsieur de Bretonvilliers had him escorted all the way by all his servants in full livery carrying torches, as befitted a prelate of his rank. The archbishop, it is said, did not call again.

The house on the corner of the rue de Bretonvilliers carries a plaque recording that the Princesse de Poix, 'très haute et très puissante', bequeathed the house in 1728 to the future Maréchal de Richelieu. The military achievements of the Maréchal (and Duc) de Richelieu, a great-nephew of the Cardinal, were against the British, notably at Port Mahon. But his greatest achievements were in bed. Even Lauzun, even Henri IV himself, could scarcely have equalled Richelieu's score. His crowd of womenfolk were distinguished not only by their number but by their variety; duchesses, servant girls, actresses, he pursued them all indefatigably. Apart from the hours spent with the ladies themselves, he devoted much time to planning how to get at them, in dealing with furious husbands, in duelling and occasionally in marrying. It is not surprising that, with such life-force, he lived till the age of ninety-two, with a final score of three wives, forty-four maîtresses en titre and an uncountable number of more informal seductions. Perhaps he was an example of Maupassant's average man who could be expected to sleep with about four hundred different women in the course of his life.

The two quais are divided by the Pont de la Tournelle, the other half, so to speak, of the Pont Marie, a modern bridge which spans the river in one white graceful spring like a flying-buttress. And from here, and from the Quai d'Orléans, we see the famous view of Notre Dame rising out of the trees, floating above the river and the city, held down by the flying-buttresses like guy-ropes. For those on the Quai d'Orléans who want something less poetic, the plain façade of the Polish Library is much admired by the British, nostalgic for Belgrave Square.

All three routes along the Île Saint-Louis join conveniently at the Brasserie de l'Île Saint-Louis, a good place to pause for a glass of Traminer or a formidable of cold beer. Nicknamed 'The Oasis', and known in earlier centuries as the Taverne du Pont Rouge, it is the island's pub. Its food and drink are Alsatian, its proprietor Monsieur Paul is a Breton and its warm pubby atmosphere makes it popular with many nations besides the French. Orders are shouted across the bar without anyone apparently taking any notice, large quantities of meals are produced in conditions of happy chaos which would make a time-and-motion study expert despair. Waiters carrying eight plates of choucroute garnie all the way up their arms to their shoulders will put them all down again to shake hands with you as you arrive. Everyone laughs, talks, jostles, and nobody is allowed to sing, not even the Germans. After a drink or a meal there, it is very hard not to have found an old friend or made a new one.

3

To reach the next island, the Île de la Cité, from the Île Saint-Louis, you have to cross the Passerelle Saint-Louis, a graceless footbridge of iron girders like a collapsed crane. It was built in 1941, a temporary replacement of the Pont Saint-Louis which had been knocked down by a barge in 1939. An earlier bridge over the same strip of the Seine, but a little nearer the tip of the Île Saint-Louis, had become dangerous in 1842. It had been built in 1819 as the previous one had become inexplicably shaky and had been closed to traffic. This had replaced the Pont Rouge (because it was painted red to protect the timbers from the weather) which

had been destroyed by floods in 1795. The Pont Rouge had been
built in 1717 on the same site as the previous bridge, which had
been knocked down by ice in 1709. The original bridge, built by
Marie, had collapsed in 1634 on its opening day, drowning twenty
and injuring forty. So far there have been eight bridges between
the two islands, a steady story of disaster.

There is a reason for this. In 1472 a group of swarthy people
were encamped beside Notre Dame. They were, it is said, a duke,
a count and ten knights, all Christian refugees from the Saracens,
from Lower Egypt, who had confessed their sins to the Pope and
been ordered as a penance to wander the world for seven years
without sleeping in a bed. With their retainers, wives, families
and children, their total reached the remarkable figure of, so it is
said, twelve hundred people, and from the descriptions of their
appearance and habits, their ear-rings, jewellery, clothes, black
hair, fortune-telling, it seems clear that they were gypsies. Their
presence annoyed the Canons of Notre Dame, and both scared
and angered the crowd. On 17 April they were driven off the
island. As they resentfully crossed in boats to the Île Notre Dame,
they cursed the strip of water beneath them.

From time to time plans are produced to replace the present
passerelle, not with a permanent stone footbridge, but with a
bridge carrying four lanes of traffic, designed to channel a non-
stop stream of heavy traffic across the tips of the two islands. The
Louisiens are tireless in signing protests against this violation of
their peace and the matter never seems to get very far. But personally I am not too worried. The gypsies' curse has never been
lifted and I am confident that any new bridge, four lanes or no,
will meet the same fate as its predecessors.

The Île de la Cité is not only the centre of Paris, the psychological centre of France. It is also the place where it all started. The
first mention of the place is in Caesar's *Gallic War*, Lutetia
Parisiorum, but it is known that the Gauls, or at least the local
tribe the Parisii, had been meeting on their island in the river long
before that, and worship on the site now occupied by Notre
Dame is as old as the island itself. Recent excavations under the
Parvis Notre Dame, in the course of making a new underground

car-park, have revealed part of a Roman wall and part of a Romanesque church, alongside each other.

The island city first seems to have been called Paris rather than Lutetia when Julian the Apostate was acclaimed emperor there in about AD 360. In 508 Clovis King of the Franks made Paris his capital and the palace of the Roman Governors (on the site now occupied by the Palais de Justice) his own palace. Here until 1360 the French kings lived, held court, dispensed justice. Here Saint Louis built the Sainte Chapelle and Philippe le Bel the Conciergerie.

Gradually Paris spread from the island on to the two banks, and now the city has a hollow centre. The Île de la Cité is no longer a place where people live, eat, drink. The centres of power, policy, commerce, learning and the arts have moved elsewhere. Only the law and the church remain, and even the archbishop no longer lives there.

At the upstream tip of the island are two gardens, both bare affairs of gravel and trees with lovely views and minimum greenery. One is on the site of the old Morgue, where corpses could arrive and leave conveniently by boat. The other is on the site of the archbishop's palace. It was until recently a forest of chestnuts, a June tapestry of white candles, red candles, young green leaves, flying-buttresses. But now most of the trees have been cut down so that they might not later become diseased, and small lime saplings have been put in their place. The garden should be a lovely fragrant place in a few hundred years' time. In the meantime it is better to walk on quickly.

Between the Quai aux Fleurs and the rue du Cloître Notre Dame is a huddle of picturesque old streets, the only part of the island to escape the great cleansing broom of Haussmann, who was trying to remove all traces of human habitation from the island. He was dismissed from his post of Prefect of the Seine before he could finish his work, but he did succeed in getting rid of twenty-five thousand people, and about ninety streets with their homes, shops and cafés.

One of the streets which has survived is the rue Chanoinesse. Despite a few old houses it is not an attractive street now, being too full of police garages and canteens. No. 10 is, however, a pleasant corner building. Not only did a comic singer live and die there some fifty years ago, as a plaque records, but in an earlier house on the same site lived Canon Fulbert and his niece Héloïse; and it was there that Abelard taught her, among other things, theology. In the taverns of the neighbouring streets, Abelard later spent, so it is said, many evenings in search of women and wine, after he had got rid of Héloïse to her nunnery and before the attack on him which rendered further evenings of this sort futile.

Turning out of the rue Chanoinesse is the rue de la Colombe, a much prettier street, ending with a picturesque restaurant once owned by the American writer Bemelmans. In the cellar of No. 5, a private house, is the old chapel of Saint-Aignan. It is an ancient place, secret, no longer a chapel. The only remains are rounded arches, columns with acanthus leaves on their capitals, a graceful plaque of the madonna, a dignified head of the saint, a well. Holy wells are usually pre-Christian, and the desolate chapel has an atmosphere not only of great age but of secrecy and forgotten mysteries.

There is, however, nothing secret nowadays about the worship in those parts. Though you cannot actually see Notre Dame from the rue Chanoinesse or the rue de la Colombe, you can feel the presence of the cathedral, you can hear the bells. Every restaurant seems to be called Esmeralda or Quasimodo, every shop seems to be selling postcards or souvenirs or transparencies of the windows, every other vehicle is a bus of tourists from Dusseldorf. For Notre Dame is not only a great cathedral; its story is the story of France, though you would never guess so from the heavily edited version put out at the son et lumière programmes.

The earliest known god to have been worshipped on the site was Cernunnos. His altar was found under Notre Dame and over thirty other sites of worship have been found elsewhere in France. Cernunnos wore antlers on his head in Herne the Hunter style and liked to sit crossed-legged on the ground, yoga fashion, a difficult position for western men and gods. He was, amongst other things, guardian of the underworld. In due course he was replaced by Jupiter, the emperor Tiberius, Saint Stephen and Our Lady.

The present building was started in 1163, a year before the death of Héloïse, and was finished in 1250. The outside glowed with colour; the statues and bas-reliefs were painted blue, scarlet, green, yellow against a background of gold. Inside was the great cavalcade of medieval life; merchants kept stalls and returned travellers showed off their souvenirs, Crusaders swore oaths, fugitives sought sanctuary and the homeless shelter. Here Saint Louis adored the truly extraordinary collection of holy relics he had acquired, and which included a feather from the wing of the Archangel Gabriel and a phial of the Virgin's milk. Here Henry IV was crowned King of England.

Unfortunately the French fell out of love with Gothic at the Renaissance. First Mansart and then Soufflot were put in to modernize the building, take out the tombs, statues, stained glass, choir stalls, rood screen and the high altar, add some neo-classical statues of virtues, whitewash the inside and generally try to turn it into a classical temple. The Revolution completed the work; the inside was sacked, and an opera dancer was enthroned as Goddess of Reason. Then the whole edifice was sold to a demolition contractor.

By the time Napoleon crowned himself emperor there, the one-time cathedral was a derelict ruin, though it was splendidly hung with tapestries for the notable occasion. In 1844, restoration at last began under Viollet-le-Duc. He replaced the spire, the statues, the windows and it is generally thought that he overdid it. But in fact his only additions were the popular gargoyles, and by the time the work was finished in 1864 Notre Dame once more resembled its medieval self as shown in the engravings.

Its ordeals were, however, not over yet. In 1871 the Communards, surely the least endearing of all revolutionaries, tried to burn it down together with all the other famous buildings of Paris. All the chairs had been heaped in the aisle, soaked with oil and set alight, when one of the incendiaries fortunately had second thoughts and put it out. In 1944 bullets whizzed about the nave during de Gaulle's Liberation Te Deum. And no doubt the story is far from finished yet.

Inside, the chief glories, apart from the springing nave, are the organ and the rose windows. One can only wonder at the single-mindedness of that great organ builder Cavaillé-Coll in constructing his masterpiece so as to block out so much of the west rose window. The other two windows, however, can be seen without any obstruction save grime. Though little of the original glass remains, the effect is still powerful. The crowds gather below them while the guide explains that though the general effect is purple, it is achieved entirely by placing red and blue glass next to each other and there is no piece of purple glass in the whole window.

'Why ever not?' exclaimed an unawestruck man. 'What's wrong with purple glass anyway?'

Outside the west doors is a large empty square, the Parvis Notre Dame. Haussmann has been severely criticized for much that he did to Paris, but for nothing more strongly than for the creation of the parvis, that paved prairie, that asphalt skating rink, as it has been called. The idea is that he spoilt the proportions of the building by allowing you to see it from too far away. You were intended, it is said, only to see it from directly underneath, peering up, cricking your neck. The original builders intended that it should rise above a picturesque huddle of old roofs, like a mother hen above her chicks.

I am doubtful whether the builders had such a romantic picture in their minds, and in any event the picturesque old houses would have long since been replaced by the usual six-storey apartment blocks; the west front would have been as invisible as the north side is today. This might have been approved in an age which prefers its cathedrals to be hidden behind modern office blocks. But standing on the Petit Pont on a winter afternoon, looking at that great façade through the bare branches, I, in my impenitent minority of one, am grateful to Haussmann for the parvis.

Perhaps the square may now be forgiven since it has acquired historic associations, the battlefield of the four-day fight between the Paris police and the German army in August 1944. And in extenuation one may add that in summer the parvis sometimes reverts to its original function as an open-air theatre for mystery plays – parvis is a corruption of paradisus.

Nothing, however, can be said in extenuation of the three huge secular buildings which were placed upon the island – the Hôtel-Dieu hospital, the Prefecture of Police and the Palais de Justice. I have never been inside two of these and hope never to have to, but a periodic visit to the Prefecture of Police is compulsory for all foreigners who live in Paris.

This is a Kafka-like experience; the endless corridors, turning a corner to reveal more corridors; dingy paint, hundreds of doors, preoccupied officials rushing to and fro carrying files, voices suddenly shouting furiously, often in a strange tongue; above all the long line of supplicants, standing, sitting, waiting, waiting. The art is to contrive (by a scraped acquaintance with Herr Klamm, say, or the Prefect's private portrait painter) to be not only priority, but super-priority, though even then a good book helps to pass the afternoon.

In fairness it must be said that it works with a good deal more efficiency than in Kafka's world, and residence permits are handed out with far more generosity than they ever were by the Castle. The girl clerks who interview you, though less forward than the Law-Court Attendant's wife or Leni, are friendly and interested. My one, who was dark and pretty, smiled sympathetically as I struggled to remember the date of my parents' wedding. 'When you write your book about the Seine, Monsieur,' she asked, 'will you mention us? The Seine is all round us.'

Gladly I put her in, for she is very much part of the river, another aspect perhaps of Sequana.

Outside the Prefecture of Police is the flower and bird market – flowers on weekdays, birds on Sundays – a gay, lively sight which almost takes your mind off the surrounding architecture. But if you have no business at the Prefecture, it is better to leave the island and cross to the left bank and plunge into the narrow winding streets of the Arab quarter. The atmosphere is very different here, the sunless streets, the dark faces, the hundreds of little restaurants offering couscous or kebabs, the cheap hotels, the dance cellars; and the sudden quick glimpses at the end of some narrow street of the cathedral across the river. We are a long way from twentieth-century Paris here, from boulevards and pavement cafés and traffic lights; we are seemingly back in the Middle Ages.

It is a shock to emerge on to the wide thoroughfare of the Boulevard Saint-Michel, not only the modern world, but a world of its own, the student world. There are many lycées and facultés in the area, and the Sorbonne is just up the street. The pavements are crowded with boys and girls, drably dressed, lugging bulging brief cases, their complexions and bearings suggesting that they are all just recovering from flu. Too much work, too much coffee, too little sleep, too little money – you do not often see in their faces the gaiety traditionally associated with the Latin Quarter. The African girls alone, with their upright carriage and their bright clothes, stand out like rainbows.

We have, however, to return to the Île de la Cité to see the Sainte-Chapelle, built by Saint Louis to house the Crown of Thorns. Whether you regard it as the supreme masterpiece of Gothic art or merely as a glasshouse with a frilly, grubby cap, it was undoubtedly a turning point in architectural history, the change from a solid and defensible building to something more delicate and etherial. The idea of a chapel wholly walled with stained glass – there are fifteen hundred square yards of it in the Sainte-Chapelle – was daring and in the Middle Ages immensely costly. By the time Pierre de Montereau finished it in 1248 it had cost eight hundred thousand livres d'or and no doubt Saint Louis thought even that too little for the sacred relic it was to house. But the chapel's effect was unquestionable; Henry III of England was overwhelmed by it.

The history of the Sainte-Chapelle is very similar to that of Notre Dame: veneration, modernization, desecration, near-demolition and finally restoration by Viollet-le-Duc. The glass was reconstructed from designs by Steinheil and little of the original remains. All the same, the experience of being inside is stunning and must be very near to what Saint Louis intended, though he would be grieved at only one service a year being held there.

I recall a concert being given there one winter night by a Yugoslav boy choir. The only light came through the windows which were floodlit from the outside; it was like being inside a jewel. Facing me, where the altar once was, was the choir, ranged like the cherubim, with clear young voices and scrubbed angelic faces, pealing out, not hymns, not carols, but a sequence of rollicking Croatian drinking songs.

To move from one extreme to the other, from human exaltation to human degradation, is only a matter of a few yards. The Conciergerie was famous for its beastliness even by the standards of medieval prisons and its vileness was not improved by the Terror. Many well-known personages stayed there briefly on their way to the guillotine or, in earlier centuries, a rather slower death. Like the Sainte-Chapelle, the Conciergerie has been modernized, restored, opened to the public and one can say once again that its impact is not what it must have been in the Middle Ages.

Behind the Palais de Justice is the small, funnel-shaped Place Dauphine. It was built to a single pattern in the early seventeenth century and many of the houses are ancient monuments. Filled with trees and quiet, it has been much admired. But it too is not what it was. Inescapably dominated by the huge Palais de Justice, solid with parked cars, I do not find it an agreeable place to linger in. I prefer to squeeze through the narrow neck of the funnel between two lovely houses of red brick and stone. There, facing me, in the middle of his bridge, rides Henricus Magnus, Henry of Navarre, the Vert Galant, Henri IV of France.

The Pont Neuf is, despite its name, the oldest bridge across the Seine. It is also the most famous, the grandest, the solidest, a triumph of bridge design. It crosses the river at its widest point in Paris, five arches across to the left bank, seven arches across to the right bank. The piers are surmounted by round bays with stone seats, for the bridge was always intended as a place for strolling and leisure. Below the rim a theatrical frieze of grimacing masks runs right round the bridge.

The bridge was not the idea of Henri IV. It had been mooted for many years without anything happening. Even when Henri II finally ordered the bridge to be built, the story remains a discouraging one. In 1578, three kings later, the first stone was at last laid by Henri III. This was a suitably gloomy occasion with the king in tears, wearing deep mourning. Some of his mignons, those screeching effeminate favourites, had been killed in the terrible triple duel a month earlier and he was still crushed with grief.

For another twenty years nothing happened and it was Henri IV in 1598 who finally ordered it to be finished. He made two notable and original changes in the design; there were to be no houses on the bridge and there were to be pavements for pedestrians. He opened the bridge himself in 1607, riding across it on his charger.

The new bridge immediately became the rendezvous of Paris. Nowadays, accustomed to strolling along boulevards and quais, it is difficult to imagine Paris as a city where it was most disagreeable to walk. The narrow streets were deep in mud and filth, jammed with wagons and horses, and rash pedestrians were barged and jostled by the lackeys of the great houses. But on the Pont Neuf Paris at last had a promenade. The bridge was in a sense the first boulevard and it would be hard to find a finer setting.

Not that it was a peaceful place. For two hundred years it was a permanent fair. Stalls and booths were set up in the round bays, traders cried their wares, singers and acrobats displayed their skills, prostitutes paraded, strolling players performed. There was a large pump called La Samaritaine which pumped water to the Louvre and which had a carillon playing every quarter of an hour. And above all there was the crowd, of all sorts and classes, endlessly moving up and down.

All this lasted until the Revolution and the Napoleonic wars. Now the fair has gone completely. The pump and the carillon have been dismantled, the traders and the jugglers and the prostitutes have moved elsewhere, the bookstalls have moved to the quais, the strollers to the boulevards. But the bridge remains, looking very much as it did on the day when Henri IV opened it, the greatest of the Seine's many bridges.

Beyond the Pont Neuf on the tip of the island, the bowsprit so to speak of the Paris ship, is the little river-level park, the Vert Galant. It is a quiet place, full of chestnut leaves and worn cobble stones and dappled light from the river; and dedicated nowadays, it would seem, to young loving couples – a thought which would have given great pleasure to the Vert Galant himself.

4

At the Pont Neuf we have to abandon our island-hopping and opt for one or other of the banks. Here I prefer the right bank. Crossing the road gingerly we plunge into the Samaritaine department store, the Seine's largest shop. The Samaritaine is very much a child of the Pont Neuf; it was named after the old pump and its founder, Monsieur Cognacq, had once cried his wares on the bridge. Prices are low, crowds are large and the usual heat would be sufficient for orchid-growing. If jugglers and prostitutes are no longer much in evidence, singers (canned) still entertain the bargain-hunters and loudspeakers cry the wares in appropriate modern phraseology: 'Madame, do you have psychological problems? Why not consult our psychiatrist on the Ground Floor, Magasin 2?'

Ignoring such temptations, we shoulder our way to the lift and go up to the roof terrace. There, around us, lies a magnificent panorama of Paris. Less lofty than the Eiffel Tower, less exhausting than the roof of Notre Dame, less remote than the Arc de Triomphe or Montmartre, the Samaritaine stands in the heart of Paris. Round us are the famous buildings, the familiar landmarks, below us the river lies glittering. On the skyline is the green line of Mont Valérien. A helpful map tells us that we are now facing Madrid.

Seen from here Paris appears to be, like Rome, a city of beautiful domes. And indeed Paris has an abundance of them: Mazarin's Institut, Richelieu's Sorbonne, Queen Anne of Austria's Val-de-Grace, Mansart's Invalides, Soufflot's Panthéon, even, if you will, the Opéra, the Sacré Coeur, the Gare de Lyon. On a summer morning, seen from the terrace, Paris seems to be blowing beautiful bubbles everywhere.

But where are the spires which should accompany and complement the domes, as the minarets complement the Blue Mosque, as Saint Mary the Virgin sets off the Radcliffe Camera? The

French, as we know from Chartres and elsewhere, are builders of wonderful spires, and medieval engravings of Paris show it as a many-steepled town, domeless and prickly. But almost all have gone now, swept away in the tide of classical fervour; Saint-Germain-des-Prés, Saint-Louis-en-l'Île, Saint-Sévérin, the spikes on Notre Dame and the Sainte-Chapelle alone remain. Perhaps the significance of Eiffel was that he restored Gothic to Paris and provided an exhilarating vertical feature in an otherwise horizontal city.

Outside the store we are on an amusing little quai, the Quai du Louvre. It is lined with shops, inside (or outside) which you may buy fishing tackle or flower bulbs, sea shells or goldfish, pet rabbits or hens. There are also some small restaurants and cafés. The traffic is normally daunting, but on Sundays or in August, when it has died down, one can enjoy from one of these cafés a fine view of the Île de la Cité, the Vert Galant, the gold-rimmed dome of the Institut, the Pont des Arts.

Or, better still, walk out into the middle of the Pont des Arts and see the water and the sky as well. The Pont des Arts is a footbridge built in 1902 of iron arches on piers of masonry. It was Paris's first iron bridge and is both enormously liked and hated, called both graceful and ugly. I find myself that it is a bridge that grows on you. Plans to replace it by a large traffic bridge seem to have been shelved, and I hope that the Pont des Arts continues a long time in its present guise – a balcony for looking at the Seine, a pitch for pavement artists, and only incidentally a way of crossing the river.

One sunny afternoon soon after I had come to live in Paris, I stopped on the Pont des Arts to admire a pavement reproduction in chalks of the Mona Lisa. It was not a very good likeness, but it was summer and I dropped five centimes into the cap. The artist, a bearded farouche young man, glowered at me.

'Take that away, monsieur, it is not enough.'

I bent down, removed my five centimes and replaced it by a ten-centime piece.

'Take that away, monsieur, it is not enough.'

I added the original five-centime piece, making fifteen centimes in all.

'Take them both away, monsieur, they are not enough.'

I asked what he charged to look at his picture.

'One franc.'

'But one can see the original in the Louvre for that!'

'Then go and see it, monsieur,' he said disagreeably.

I decided to take his advice, but further along the bridge I was attracted by a yellow and black tachiste painting. Its artist was equally bearded and farouche, but his manner was gentler and he was, I thought, a good deal more talented. So I bought his picture for a few francs, carried it home, framed it and hung it just inside the front door of my flat. But, alas, the comments of my friends – 'I never knew you owned a Pollock' – showed that I was giving a false impression of my financial position, and I eventually felt obliged to move it.

5

On the Quai du Louvre or the Pont des Arts I get the feeling I sometimes feel at a cocktail party: I am having an interesting and enjoyable talk and out of the corner of my eye I can see the party's bore waiting to move in and take over. As I stand there enjoying the Seine, the bâteaux-mouches, the river fire-brigades with their gleaming brass, it is difficult not to be uncomfortably aware of the Louvre.

The statistics of the Louvre are well known. It is the largest palace on earth. It houses a magnificent collection of art treasures, many of which come from other lands than France. It was started by King Philippe Auguste in 1202 and finished by the Emperor Napoleon III in 1868, six hundred and sixty-six years later. Seventeen sovereigns, dozens of architects were involved in its construction. It spans the history of France from medieval fortress to Second Empire folly.

On and on it goes beside the Seine, mile after mile (so it seems), façade after façade, relentlessly dignified and mediocre, its clean golden stone showing only too clearly that it was never touched by architectural genius; neither a masterpiece nor a historic monument; merely old and grandiose.

The trouble with the Louvre is that, in the long and turbulent history of France, so little happened there. So few of France's rulers lived there. The Louvre was a palace they paid lip-service to; each one added another wing, a gallery, a pavilion, another domino or two to the ground-plan, while preferring to be somewhere else. Saint Louis lived on the Île de la Cité, Henri II in the Tournelle, Catherine de Medici in the Tuileries, Marie de Medici in the Luxembourg, Louis XIV at Saint-Germain and Versailles, Napoleon at the Tuileries and Fontainebleau, his nephew at the Tuileries, de Gaulle at the Elysée. Catherine de Medici and Louis XIV lived for a while in the Louvre while they awaited the completion of the Tuileries and Versailles respectively. Francois I was there under protest, one of the conditions made by the Parisians for paying his ransom.

The only monarchs who seem to have lived in the Louvre for choice were the sons of Catherine de Medici, mignons and all, Henri IV who died there, and his son Louis XIII once he had escaped from his mother and the Luxembourg.

Centuries of royal boredom have done something to the building, to its very stones; the place glows with boredom and the sensitive passer-by cannot but be aware of it. It is for this reason, of course, that the palace still survives. Nobody has ever cared enough about it to burn it down; even the Communards were half-hearted when it came to the Louvre.

In order to avoid acquiring a cafard most unsuitable both to Paris and the Seine, it is therefore better to remain, after the Pont des Arts, on the left bank, the Quai Malaquais and the Quai Voltaire. Here is a pleasant line of eighteenth-century houses and the enjoyment of looking at them is much increased by recalling what a distinguished collection of writers, painters and composers lived here beside the Seine, sometimes briefly, sometimes for long periods: Anatole France (at 19 Quai Malaquais), Ingres (11 Quai Voltaire), Delacroix and Corot (at No. 13 in the same studio, but not together), Baudelaire, still gazing at the Seine, Wagner, finishing *Die Meistersinger*, and Oscar Wilde, in exile, all in the hotel at

No. 19, though not of course together. Voltaire himself was at No. 27 in 1724, aged thirty. Fifty-four years later, after years of exile, he returned in triumph to the same house and died a few weeks later.

6

Walking along the quai we must pause to admire the simple grace of the Pont Royal, Louis XIV's gift to the Seine. Paris has been unlucky in many of her bridges, but the three oldest have a sense of curve, a dignity and a beauty which was later forgotten; to be remembered again in this century, judging from the most modern bridge, the Pont de la Tournelle.

On our left is the dark hulk of the Gare d'Orsay, once the gateway to south-west France and Spain. Even at the height of nineteenth-century railway fever it must have seemed an odd place to build a mainline station, a reckless squandering of central space and Seine frontage. It is now virtually derelict, used for such unlikely activities as film-making; Orson Welles shot his version of Kafka's *The Trial* in its sombre caverns. It is soon to be demolished and replaced by a modern hotel, whose guests should enjoy a lovely view of the river, the Pont Royal and the Tuileries Gardens on the other bank.

We also pass, moored in the river, one of Paris's few swimming pools, the Piscine Deligny. The idea of a floating pool is an intriguing one, and its water is filtered and drinkable, unlike that of its mother river. It has been there since 1842.

At the end of the Quai Anatole France, we must of course turn right on to the Pont de la Concorde. There before us lies the Place de la Concorde, the great square, famous for its size, its splendour and its beauty. I have to confess myself one of its less entranced admirers. The gibes which have been levelled at the Parvis Notre Dame apply a hundred times more to this huge square, which dwarfs the surrounding buildings. Filled with fountains, statues, electric lamps, flagstaffs, hundreds of hooting cars and an Egyptian obelisk, it still remains a paved prairie. It cries out for some vertical feature more solid than the obelisk, a building loftier and nobler than the pair on the north side – a cathedral, say – to give the square a focus and a purpose.

The square was finished in 1763 from designs by Gabriel, who also built the two buildings on the north side. These are also widely regarded as masterpieces. With their columns and pediments they continue deliberately the façades of the Louvre to the culminating point of French classical architecture. But again I am less impressed than I should be. It is not so much their derivativeness, their unoriginality which jars as their shamness. Though they now house a ministry, a hotel and the French Automobile Club, they are not really buildings at all. They are mere façades, scenery, two-dimensional backdrops intended to be seen from the front only. Even while he was designing and building them Gabriel had no idea what they were to be used for.

Standing on the Pont de la Concorde it is said that you can see more classical columns than from any single point in either Athens or Rome. The longing of the French to fill their capital with large Roman temples went on for a long time, and Napoleon was only one enthusiast. I do not know who first pronounced the law that if you copy the architecture of a different civilization two thousand years later, even if you alter the size and proportions, you automatically produce a masterpiece. But many Frenchmen do regard the final products as masterpieces, even surpassing in beauty the originals that inspired them. André Maurois went so far as to write: 'There is not on this planet a more beautiful architectural ensemble than that which leads from the Arc de Triomphe to the Louvre and from the Madeleine to the Palais Bourbon.'

The Roman temple of the Chambre des Deputés is a complete sham. Not even a half temple, it is only a Corinthian façade stuck on to the back of the Palais Bourbon, whose main entrance is the other side. Across the square, up the perspective of the rue Royale, is the twin temple, the Madeleine. This at least is no façade, but a large solid building which can be seen from all sides, a puffed-up Maison Carrée. Moreover, it was actually built with a purpose in mind, the glorification of the Grande Armée, though this purpose had evaporated long before the building was finished. One can imagine the problem of the French in 1842 in finding a use for the brand-new Roman temple in their midst. As a church it was (and is) a discouraging place, pagan and windowless. The Grande Armée was already fully glorified in the Arc de Triomphe and the Invalides. As a railway station, another suggestion, it was too small. The same objection applied to earlier suggestions for using the site for the Banque de France or the Bourse or the Bibliothèque Nationale. Indeed, the Madeleine is really only suited for the worship of Jupiter or as a cinema, and it was two thousand years too late for one and a hundred years too early for the other.

But despite Napoleon, despite Gabriel, despite the grandeur that never was Rome, the Place de la Concorde remains a thrilling place. One does not cross it without a shiver of excitement, a shiver not only due to the tumultuous traffic. Unlike the Louvre much has happened there and it only needs a modest imagination to see again the tumbrils, the tricoteuses and, on the site now occupied by the statue of Strasbourg, the blade of the guillotine going up and down, up and down. And the story does not stop with the end of the Terror: Napoleon's funeral in 1840, the riots of 1848 when the mob shouted 'In two hours we will sack all Paris', the Stavisky riots of 1934, the silent deserted square in the dark days of 1940 with the sky black with the smoke of burning oil depots, the fighting during the liberation of the city, the delirious welcome given to de Gaulle a few hours later.

It is a violent story which, like that of Notre Dame, is still unfinished. But the Place de la Concorde has, appropriate to its name, more peaceful pleasures: to come out of the Jeu de Paume gallery, the mind's eye still full of Monet and Pissarro, and see big clouds sailing across a wide autumn sky; to stand there on a wet night and watch the lights – there are over two hundred of them – reflected in the shiny road, and the red tail-lights of cars shimmering up the Champs Elysées; to pass through on a May morning when the gardens at either side are filled with such a great flood of fresh spring green.

There is more to the Place de la Concorde even than that. So many millions of visitors have come there almost as pilgrims, seeing it as the heart of gay Paris, have stared goggle-eyed up the famous trompe-l'oeil perspective of the Champs Elysées, and their thrill has rubbed off on to the square itself, has impregnated it, transformed it. The excitement that I feel there has nothing to do with eyesight. I would know where I was blindfold.

7

The Pont de la Concorde is an austere plain bridge, unremarkable in every way. It does not draw the eye from its famous surroundings. It merely carries traffic. The same cannot be said of the next bridge down, the Pont Alexandre III. True, it carries its fair share of traffic, but it is the most sumptuous, the most flamboyant of all the Seine's bridges. Every spare centimetre is encrusted with decoration: cupids, scrolls, garlands of flowers, wreaths, shells, birds, shields, trumpets, lions – they are all there, some in stone, some in bronze, some gilded.

Its only architectural relation would seem to be the Opéra, which had been finished twenty-five years earlier. And indeed the Empress Eugénie's comment on being shown the designs for the Opéra – 'But what style is this meant to be?' – can be applied as well to the Pont Alexandre III. And the answer would be very similar. It is the style of the Third Republic, and it is unique.

But though it clamours for much attention, it does not often get it. For this part of Paris is not an area for leisurely strolling, for the flâneur. The bookstalls have gone; loving couples, children, pavement cafés, pedestrians are few. The left bank at river level is already an express motor road. You do not walk about this area, you drive very fast. Even the tourists, dashing in their taxis from the Emperor's tomb to lunch on the Eiffel Tower and on to the Champs Elysées, do not usually have time to stand and stare at the Seine and its bridges.

There are many attractions in this part of Paris, for visitors with specialized interests as well as routine tourists: the motor show at the Grand Palais, the salons at the Musée d'Art Moderne, the dress shows at the fashion houses, the concerts at the Théatre des Champs Elysées or the Palais de Chaillot. This is a world of luxury hotels and expensive restaurants and smart night clubs. Gay Paree may still be centred on Pigalle or Montmartre or the Champs Elysées, but Tout-Paris remains beside or near the river.

As we drive fast down one of the quais (for the time for walking is past), we can catch a glimpse on our left of the Invalides, the Valhalla of French soldiers. If we happen to be going to the Air Terminal, which is under the Esplanade, we may have the chance of a longer look. The Esplanade des Invalides is yet another imposing vista, another paved prairie and this time the biggest of them all. But at the far end, above the dignified façade of the seventeenth-century Hotel des Invalides, floats Mansart's big beautiful golden bubble, the finest dome in Paris and worthy of the vast acreage in front of it.

The next landmark is, of course, the Eiffel Tower, bestriding the Champs de Mars in four great springing arches. It has, ever since it was first planned for the 1889 exhibition, been derided for its monstrosity, its ugliness and its pointlessness. An architect once told me that it was one of the most beautiful buildings in the world, a masterpiece of curved grace and lightness and proportion. But then, he explained, Eiffel was luckier than most architects; he had a thousand feet of height at his disposal and only three storeys to fit in. If these could have been reduced to two, the building would have been perfect. The most common reaction, however, is now neither admiration nor hate, but an amused affection. Is there anyone still left in the world who wants it pulled down?

Facing the tower across the river is another unusual building, the Palais de Chaillot, also built for an exhibition, that of 1937. It consists of two wings to a building without the building, and it does not find many admirers. But it stands on a hill and from its terrace you get a fine view of Paris and the Seine. Inside, it houses several museums including the Musée de l'Homme, and a large theatre where the Théatre National Populaire performs famous plays for relatively modest prices.

Below the Palais are gardens and fountains, and from here fire-works are let off on nights of national celebration. On 8 May 1965 I stood on the bridge, one of a vast crowd gaping and saying 'Ooh-ah' at the showers of golden rain in the black sky, the reflections in the black river. There were, I believe, over a hundred thousand of us in the area at that time and for once we were all, or almost all, on foot.

Below the Palais de Chaillot the Seine becomes something of a frontier and the difference between the two banks is very marked. On the left is Grenelle, a grimy working-class area full of factories and builders' yards and rubbish tips. Much of the river-front is taken up by the Citroen factory, and the rest seems to be occupied by barges loading sand or cement or rubble, by railway yards and small shabby houses.

Facing Grenelle across the river are the white modern blocks of the Seizième, the sixteenth arrondissement. This is the beau quartier, the fashionable area, the equivalent of Eaton Square in London or the East Sixties in New York. Here are the great houses with their huge salons, their wide stone staircases, their gardens full of trees and classical statues; and now usually divided into large flats. Among them are the modern blocks, the appartements de grand *standing*, still large and luxurious with fast lifts and terraces and little patches of lawn with modern fountains. You have to be rich to live in the Seizième and its inhabitants are very proud of their address. An invitation to a party there implies your best clothes and champagne and talk about Mediterranean villas and faraway airports.

The Seizième begins at the busy Pont d'Alma and continues, a prosperous hillside of apartment blocks and wide streets and big cars, all the way to Auteuil, stretching away as far as the Étoile and the Bois de Boulogne. It ends at the city limits. The Seizième is the end of the Seine in Paris. When the river reaches Auteuil it is seven miles longer than it was at Charenton, much dirtier and infinitely more glamorous.

Part Three: Downstream

1

I left the Quai des Invalides early one Sunday morning in May on the yacht G. *Borde Fretigny*, a vessel papered with documents and photographs proving that the Queen once sailed on her through Paris. It was a dark, chilly morning and I wished I had brought a thicker coat. The other passengers came aboard, looking equally green, glanced hurriedly round them and then buried their noses in last Wednesday's edition of *France-Dimanche*. A little rain pattered on the windows. Slowly we pulled out and turned round till we were pointing downstream, seawards.

Round us everything was quiet. There was hardly any traffic along the quais; the bâteaux-mouches and the private yachts which moor for the night on these quays were silent and deserted. Paris, both Grenelle and the Seizième, was still asleep. No cranes moved by the gravel heaps, nobody appeared on the balconies of the appartements de grand *standing*. Even the children of the other passengers were subdued. I yawned.

It is difficult to work up much excitement about the Seine as it leaves Paris. After the Citroen works come the Renault works. Of course car factories are important and interesting places, but what can anyone say for the long derelict island between them, which seems mainly to be used as a rubbish tip? Why not turn it into a modern Île Saint-Louis, I wondered. In overcrowded land-hungry Paris, why not clear it and build some attractive modern apartment blocks of only moderately grand standing? Why not mend the windows, cut down the weeds, use the place? But this was still the Seine, I reminded myself, the beautiful romantic historic Seine which had started as a sacred trickle and had turned into a song-soaked lake under the bridges of Paris, but whose chief interest is as an industrial waterway. And though Saint-Cloud may not look very prepossessing just now, it looks wonderful at night with all the neon reflected in the water. And that eighteenth-century building on the left is Madame de Pompadour's porcelain factory at Sèvres, and anyway Sisley thought the Seine was good enough to paint, both at Sèvres and Suresnes.

I was rewarded for my dogged optimism. There was a sudden vision behind Sèvres of a hillside covered with beeches and chestnuts in full candle. On the right were more chestnuts, exploding like fireworks, a sailing club gay with flags and bunting, a camp full of coloured tents. Beyond was the Bois de Boulogne. As we slid into the Suresnes lock, I felt as if I had arrived in open country. Well, that wasn't too bad, I said to myself, the industrial wilderness didn't last long. How wrong I was!

At the Pont de Neuilly we passed under the longest straight city street in France, which starts at the Maison de la Défense at Courbevoie, goes across the Seine, under the Arc de Triomphe, and down to the Place de la Concorde, a street only surpassed in length by Fifth Avenue. Neuilly-sur-Seine, as a Paris suburb, is an odd place today. The older houses are still lived in by the old families, and the greengrocers still say, 'Henri, two kilos of potatoes for the marquise and a ripe melon for the vicomtesse.' On top of this has arrived a flood of Arabs from North Africa, who pester the marquises as they stroll beside the Seine and will no doubt drive them soon to the Seizième. On the left bank rise, among astoundingly ugly houses, some huge blocks of flats, plain, severe, but interesting, and perhaps these will become the home of the stable middle-class element that Neuilly so badly needs.

At Neuilly starts the long island of La Grande Jatte, the subject of Seurat's picture, probably the most famous of all pointilliste pictures, a marvel of sunlight and brilliant water and glowing colour, all built up from thousands of dots. But La Grande Jatte doesn't look like that now. The life and the colour have gone, together with the parasols, the ladies in bustles, the pet monkeys, the oarsmen. Apart from a small neo-classical temple at the Neuilly end and a few hard tennis courts, the island is not a place for leisure. Tipped rubbish, shabby warehouses, disused sheds – even Seurat, even in sunshine, would find it hard to find colour there any more.

The stretch of the Seine from Neuilly to Chatou is arguably the

most unpleasing stretch of river-front in the world, and coming
so soon after the glorious Paris miles, the effect is startling and
saddening. As we moved through the flat featureless landscape,
past the Saint-Denis locks, past the entrance of the port of
Gennevilliers, past small derelict factories with broken windows,
past mile after mile of banks filthy with refuse, I wondered if anything more possibly could be done to make this stretch uglier.
The redeeming factor is the great sweeping bend of the river at
Saint-Denis, but like the other bends between Paris and Mantes,
this is more spectacular on the map than on the site. You are only
aware that you have passed Levallois-Perret and now reached
Colombes by the fact that the distant Eiffel Tower, which was
first to port and then to starboard, is now to port again.

In the middle of this desolate waste we passed the town of
Argenteuil. Argenteuil! Probably the most painted town in history after Venice. How well we know that little white square,
that steeple, that bridge, that river-front, that flat landscape! How
often have we smiled at the inhabitants of Argenteuil, those
walrus-moustached men in striped vests and boaters, those bourgeois women in boats, wearing big straw hats and veils so
unsuitable for aquatics. And behind it all the river – so deep blue,
so silver-blue, so green-grey, so dappled with reflections of poplars and walls and clouds, so flecked with sails and oarsmen and
regatta bunting and flags. And above everything the luminous
skies of the Île-de-France, the sailing clouds, the sunlight. Was it
never bad weather at Argenteuil? Did it never rain on that stretch
of the Seine? Did they never have dark drizzling mornings like
today? Well, we know that it snowed at Louveciennes and
flooded at Port-Marly and unsettled weather sometimes showed
in the sky over the distant factory chimney. But in general there
was sunlight over everything, sunlight in the eye of the painter,
excitement in his breast.

The Impressionists (they never called themselves this, it was a
term of abuse used by the critics and the public) moved into
Argenteuil in 1871, after the war, though Monet had been there
before. Renoir, Sisley, Degas and Caillebotte joined him there, to
be followed by Manet, the doyen of the group, and Berthe

Morisot. For ten years they painted the streets, the river, the people and each other, sharing their enthusiasms and despairs, painting almost always out of doors, trying to capture the melting colours, the shifting lights. Nearby at Pontoise were Pissarro and Cézanne. It was one of the most successful mutual admiration societies in history, and one of the most fully justified.

What was it that drew these painters to this part of France, to the Seine and its tributaries? No doubt it was partly convenience, a flat open countryside near enough to Paris to be readily access-ible. And it was partly the light, the gentle luminous skies of the Seine valley, the soft shadows, the colours unbleached by too bright a sun. But it was chiefly the Seine itself that attracted them, so wide, so slow, sometimes rippled, sometimes glassy, always reflecting the sky and the boats and the trees. This they would not have found beside the sandy Loire or the turbulent Rhône, romantic though these rivers are. But then the Impressionists were not wanting to be romantic, they were reacting from romantic painting. It is only we who find them romantic in retrospect.

In 1880 the group began to break up, to go their separate ways: Monet went to Vétheuil and Giverny, Sisley to Moret, the others back to Paris or to the hot glare of the south. And Argenteuil gradually turned into an industrial suburb of Paris, as dismal and grimy as any. There are warehouses now along the waterfront, factories dominate the bridge; and, though Monet was never one to mind a distant smudge of factory smoke, I do not think any painters could find luminosity there today. Or again perhaps they could. Perhaps Argenteuil was never as delightful as they made it seem. Perhaps the radiance was only ever in their brushes.

Morose with thoughts like these, I bought myself some coffee at the bar. The other passengers still had their faces firmly inside *France-Dimanche*. I wished that I had brought a copy with me.

2

At Bougival everything suddenly changed. Abruptly we were out of industrial grime into green countryside. On the left was a hillside covered with trees, fresh green beeches, copper beeches, white-candled chestnuts, pink-candled chestnuts, oaks, sycamores, all unpollarded, unclipped, unurbanized. The village of Bougival itself is delightful, a water-front of old houses beside the lock, among the trees, under the hill. Across the bridge was a small restaurant, the 'Robinson', with a garden terrace facing the river. It was the first riverside restaurant I had seen since Paris.

At this enjoyable moment, as we slowed for the lock, the sun burst through the clouds and it was a fine day. I loved Bougival at first sight and I promised myself that I would return later by land and explore the place. It is a promise I have kept several times.

The 'Robinson' is on an island; indeed, it was the first building there, hence the name. It is calm and peaceful, there is no traffic, nothing between you and the rippling water. The house was painted by Renoir, the canopy of chestnut leaves overhead is a hundred years old. What could be pleasanter on a summer's day than to sit there and move effortlessly back into a Manet picture? I unbutton my blazer to show my striped vest, stroke my moustache, ogle the lady at the next table and watch the light pouring through a glass of Aligoté.

And who are all those gay young people making such a noise at the landing stage, boating, bathing, splashing, laughing? Surely they must be the canotiers, having the time of their lives. And that young sculler pulling his boat into the side, eyeing the girls, isn't that Monsieur de Maupassant, Flaubert's friend? And that little island by the landing stage, that must be La Grenouillère. And those two figures on the bank behind the easels, both painting the lively scene, they seem familiar. But of course, the one on the left, under the big hat, is Monsieur Renoir, the one on the right Monsieur Monet. How different the two pictures look! The

Monet one is about water and boats and reflections, while the Renoir one is about the people. And that figure in the distance, with his back turned to the rest of us, that must be the Englishman, Mr Sisley. You can recognize him by his sabots, he is too poor to buy shoes. There aren't any people in his picture, only water and trees and sky.

But what is that sound coming across the river? Not a radio surely, not in the nineteenth century. It must be Monsieur Berlioz, sitting in his room in the inn, humming his new march. Oh, he's stopped now, Monsieur Corot must have called up to him to be quiet.

The dream, the chronology seems to have got rather out of control. No matter. Madame Paulette, another glass of Aligoté, please. And is canard aux olives on your menu today? It is? Excellent.

The idyll is alas threatened. The idea is to pull down the restaurant, cut down the chestnuts, and build a new bridge across the Seine, carrying a new main road through Bougival to connect with the autoroute beyond Louveciennes. But the impressionist dream can still be dreamed beside the river under the aged willows of the 'Auberge du Fruit Défendu' a few hundred yards upstream.

Or for a change you can try Port-Marly, a little further on. There is a large yacht-club here and the river on Sundays flashes with colour; white sails, red sails, blue stripes, green stripes, happy young canotiers in their yellow life-jackets, waving. You have a choice of two restaurants at Port-Marly; one serves Île-de-France food, the other Provençale. Neither seems to be the inn so spectacularly flooded in Sisley's 'Inondations', with its white wall advertising Nicolas wines standing up squarely against the wet sky. Just as well, as this for once is not a scene I would be happy to relive.

Beyond Port-Marly, beyond the river bend, rises the old town of Saint-Germain-en-Laye on its hill. There is in fact little to be seen from the river. But the view from the top, from the terrasse, is magnificent. To the left, on the edge of the escarpment, stretches the great terrace, one and a half miles long, flanked on one side by old lime trees and on the other side by air. It was constructed in 1673 on the orders of Louis xiv and is one of Le Nôtre's triumphs. Ahead lies the great view of Paris and the Seine valley. In the 'Pavillon Henri iv', facing this view, Louis xiv was born on 5 September 1658. Perhaps that vast panorama reached those infant eyes and the idea lodged then in that immature brain that Europe lay there awaiting his conquest and devastation.

The room still looks very much as it must have during that momentous parturition, apart from some chairs of later date. It has been incorporated in a hotel, which has housed a number of famous people, inspired by that view to more creative activity. There Offenbach and Delibes composed, and Dumas wrote *The Three Musketeers*. You can lunch there now, sensationally though not cheaply.

Behind the terrasse is the château itself, that strange amalgam of styles, hardly beautiful but full of interest. It was Louis xiv's favourite residence, until he decided that he preferred a place without any previous history, and moved to Versailles.

But Saint-Germain has many royal associations other than with Louis xiv. Unlike the Louvre, much happened there. It was a fortress in the twelfth century and later a castle, a refuge from the tumultuous Paris mob. Saint Louis built another Sainte-Chapelle there, which is still a beautiful building though it has now no stained glass and is only half its proper length. In Saint-Germain many kings were born, married or died. Mary Queen of Scots passed her childhood there, and married her first husband, the boy dauphin. James ii passed his exile there. But perhaps the jolliest time in the palace's history was when Henri iv parked fourteen of his children there, together with their various mothers. It was an ingenious, though possibly noisy, solution of his particular problem.

After Saint-Germain we passed another small town, Maisons-Laffitte with its château which was yet another royal residence. But the place is better known to Parisians today for its race-course. Behind it and round it is the vast green carpet of the forest of Saint-Germain, but the hill, the escarpment was gone. The hill was now on the right, at Herblay, as we banked round on

our next bend to the left. For this part of the Seine is rather like a
bob-run, if such a simile were not unseemly for such a slow and
stately river.

The hillside at Herblay was dotted with rather ugly villas, but
at least they were looking at and enjoying the river, something
which I had not found further up. The left bank was green with
the forest and the water was blue and dotted with sails. It was all
rather like a Swiss lake.

Still on the same left-hand bend we reached Conflans-Sainte-
Honorine, where the Seine is joined by the Oise. This is one of
the Seine's great traffic junctions, straight on for Rouen and Le
Havre, turn right for Belgium and Holland. Conflans itself is the
Saint-Mammès of the lower Seine, its quais lined with barges, five
or six deep. Others were on the move and I suspected these were
driven by their owners, like *Sacolève*, who cannot afford Sunday
off. Above them fluttered their washing like flags, dozens of pairs
of children's knickers, for the owner's wife too works on Sunday.
But the parked barges, belonging to the big companies, were
motionless, though not exactly silent. No washing hung above
these decks, for Madame takes Sunday off too. I suppose she has
larger reserves of knickers for her children.

Conflans, like Saint-Mammès, is given over to the needs of
bargees and is populated by retired mariners. Several old barges
have been converted into rather ramshackle houseboats, one
looking like a Noah's Ark. The barge called appropriately *Jesers*
serves as a chapel for bargees. Though there is a fine twelfth-
century church on top of the hill, no bargee would willingly go
on shore, even for his devotions, even on a Sunday when he is not
going anywhere.

The junction of the two rivers is a tranquil, pastoral affair,
without embankments or factories. Afterwards the Seine was
wider, statelier than ever. The atmosphere on board too changed
at Conflans. They brought us aperitifs, hors-d'œuvres, lunch,
wine. My fellow passengers put away *France-Dimanche*, opened
their napkins and began to talk animatedly. But I was still the
only one who looked out.

3

The stretch of a dozen miles from Poissy to Meulan I recall with delight. The countryside was beautiful, the waterfront pretty, the gigot d'agneau excellent. This part of the Seine is a commuters' area, and a week-end pleasure garden. The Seine dominates everyone's life; fishing, boating, sailing are the leisure occupations of almost everyone. Each house has its lawns running down to the river, its landing stage, its boathouse. Indeed, some of the boathouses were actually lived in.

Trees are everywhere: an avenue of old limes at Poissy, willows weeping into the water on the edges of lawns, poplars guarding the long island at Villennes like sentries, green beeches, copper beeches, the hillside at Triel gaudy with purple and white lilac; and above all, chestnuts, chestnuts everywhere, hundreds of them, all of them in full candle, pink candle, white candle. How many candles did I see that day? Millions, I think.

The villages are pretty too, Villennes, Medan, Triel, with their little squares beside the river and their old houses. Under the trees people were lunching in restaurants called 'La Frégate' or 'La Marine' or 'Le Coq au Vin'. They watched us as we steamed by and I hoped they were enjoying their lunch as much as I was.

Poissy itself is more than a village; it is more of an industrial town, though this does not show from the river. Saint Louis was born there and he sometimes used to sign letters Louis de Poissy. But I do not think he would recognize much there now except perhaps a few stones in the church. The building which dominates Poissy now is the Simca car factory, a huge erection, but neat, clean, shining; a pleasure to see after some of the factories we had passed earlier. Car factories are a feature of the lower Seine. At Elisabethville, near Meulan, there are fields and fields of cars like a crop, like mushrooms sprouted after rain.

The afternoon's races seemed on the point of starting and the river was alive with coloured sails and fluttering burgees and club flags. The dinghies had crews of two, a sporting young man at the helm, a pretty girl crewing, both wearing yellow life-jackets, both sitting well out of their boats in the breeze. I fear we must have got dreadfully in their way as they manoeuvred at the start line in front of the judges' box, but they did not seem to mind us. Perhaps they were used to such hazards; after all, the petrol barges of the Union Normande went to and fro across their course every other minute. There were larger yachts, with striped spinnakers, out for a sail, and motor boats turning the chestnut reflections into arrow patterns.

The sporting life reaches its climax at Meulan where the river is particularly wide and joined by two small tributaries. For those who need even more space for their pleasure, there is an airstrip for light aircraft.

But beyond Meulan there is an abrupt change. The landscape remains pastoral, but industry has recovered its grip on the river again. The hills on either side are scarred with quarries, the one on the left enormous like a moon crater. On either bank are big cement factories, connected to the quarries by overhead cable railways like chair-lifts. A white mist hangs over the factories, dusting the factory roofs, the parked cars, the waiting barges, the surface of the river. From a chemical works a sulphurous fragrance came between me and my Camembert, transporting me in the wrinkling of a nose to Lancashire; and happily back again. At Porcheville was another big Centrale d'Electricité, with two tall chimneys and a huge tip of coal slack. Opposite was another cement factory. And round and behind everything were the poplars and the fields and the woods of the valley. It was an incongruous mixture.

Then abruptly ahead of us we saw our cruise's end, Mantes-la-Jolie, its great church with its pierced towers and flying buttresses – almost a cathedral – standing magnificently on its rise above the river. The yacht moored alongside the bank and we straggled ashore to stretch our legs and buy postcards.

4

I had been at Mantes-la-Jolie before. Exactly four weeks earlier I had wandered round the town in the company of two charming Parisian friends, the Boverat sisters. It was a wonderful spring morning, silver clouds ballooned across a pale blue sky, and the fruit trees in the orchards were loaded with blossom. It was Palm Sunday and the streets were full of people carrying branches of box, Birnam Wood coming to church.

Mantes-la-Jolie has had rather a stormy history. William the Conqueror claimed the town in 1087 as part of his endless quarrel with the French king. The king, Philippe I, refused, making some ribald remarks about the size of William's stomach. 'No woman in Normandy has been in child-bed as long as fat William. It will take many candles to relieve him of his burden.' William retorted that he would light a hundred thousand candles at the expense of the king of France. He took Mantes and burnt it to the ground, including the church. But while he rode round the town, enjoying the blaze, his horse trod on a hot cinder and William was badly injured in his lower stomach by the pommel of the saddle. He died of gangrene in Rouen six weeks later. The accident, he thought, was all due to burning down the church, and he left orders and money for it to be rebuilt.

In due course not only a new church but a fine new town, Pretty Mantes, rose from the ashes. Its second destruction took place during the last war. It was damaged in 1940, but the real bombardment was in the spring of 1944. The allied plan for the Normandy battle involved sealing off the battlefield from German reinforcements by destroying every bridge over the Seine below Paris. I was to find sad evidence of this plan all the way to Rouen. In Mantes the church was spared this time, but the rest of the old town fell under the bombs, and few old houses now remain. The church of Saint-Maclou, however, was destroyed during the Revolution.

The rebuilding has been done in sober local stone, the houses being of the same style but in different designs and heights, and the effect is quite pleasing. Care has been taken to preserve the amphitheatre of the hillside and the view across the river.

Henri IV was particularly fond of Mantes-la-Jolie, or, more exactly perhaps, of Gabrielle d'Estrées who lived there. It was in Mantes that he made his famous decision to renounce Protestantism in May 1595. In tears he said to his friend and minister the Duc de Sully, 'Que veux tu, if I refuse to renounce, there will be no more France', a sentence which is usually misquoted as the more cynical and self-seeking 'Paris is worth a mass'.

Few ministers in history have been abler and more faithful to their masters than Sully. He was born at Rosny, some four miles downstream from Mantes, and in the same year that Henri made his renunciation, Sully began to build himself a château at Rosny. Steep-roofed, the walls brick and stone, with the simple unadorned style of the time, it looks much better than in Corot's drab little picture. But Sully's chief interest was less the house than the park, the avenue, the terrace beside the Seine, the gardens. He planted eight thousand mulberry trees on his estate, but to help raise money for his master's wars he cut down the whole of the forest of Rosny and sold the timber. After the murder of Henri IV he could not bear to continue building and gardening, and all work was stopped. He and Henri had often been there together, and now in his sadness he abandoned the work unfinished.

We followed the riverside road from Rosny to Rolleboise, a delightful village on the edge of the river and once the terminus of the galiote fluviale, the water-bus drawn by four horses, which went from here to Poissy. Above the village is a steep hill, and at the top is the Corniche road and a restaurant with a view. However, we preferred to stay by the river, to sit in the spring sunshine on the terrace of the 'Hostellerie La Ruche' and have a drink and talk and contemplate the blossom and the river at leisure.

The Seine is a different river below Paris. It has changed its name again and is now officially at last La Seine. It is wider and dirtier. Though it still reflects the blue sky, there is oil and scum on the surface, and clouds of pollution drift about below. Of the river's most characteristic inhabitants, the fishermen are still there but the washerwomen have gone altogether. But the sportsmen and the barges remain. There are more petrol barges on this stretch and it has been called the River of Petrol. Despite the pipe-line from Le Havre to Paris, there is still plenty of water-borne traffic, carrying oils which are not suitable for the pipeline. Up and down they go, high out of the water going downstream, and coming upstream so low in the water that it splashes the deck; barges of the fleet of the Union Normande with their smart alu-minium paint and their complicated pipes and valves and their notices stating in three languages that smoking is forbidden. How did a bargee manage, I wondered, if he happened to be a com-pulsive chain-smoker?

'Do you know Napoleon's phrase?' asked Marguerite Boverat. 'He said that Paris, Rouen and Le Havre are one town and the Seine is its main street.'

But there are still many familiar things about the Seine here. It is still glassy, full of reflections, unhurried, seeming to move gently upstream or downstream as the mood takes it. It still prefers to wander about the valley rather than head for the sea.

One of the most beautiful of its loops is just beyond Rolleboise. The inside of the bend, the convex side, is flat with a forest. The outside bank, the concave side, has a steep escarpment or chalk down. The spurs have broken off to form small white triangular cliffs which are such a feature of the valley, first on one side and then on the other as the river coils to and fro between them. On reaching the first cliffs at La Roche Guyon, the Seine turns about and heads the opposite way. By the time that it reaches Bonnières, thirteen miles downstream from Rolleboise, it is still only two miles away from Rolleboise across the hill.

Far from trying to reach the sea, the Seine's chief objective is to wash away the escarpments, the cliffs, and deposit the chalk as silt on the inside of the next bend. Far from cutting the corners, the idea is to enlarge the loops. At first sight this seems rather a dreary objective, flattening the landscape, altering the course, lengthen-ing the river. But in fact the wish of the Seine to curl and loop and meander, which is its principal characteristic, is also its great blessing. A slow winding river drains the countryside very gently, leaving it lush and fertile. A straight fast river drains the valley rapidly producing aridity. How the farmers of the Seine valley must hope that no fanatical engineer ever tries to straighten the river, to cut off the loops. The Celtic word for 'twisting', they say, is squan; and Sequana is the twisting goddess.

5

La Roche-Guyon has perhaps the most peculiar château on the whole Seine. It started with a dungeon or keep built on and inside the cliff, high above the river, constructed in the eleventh century. In due course a house was built at the foot of the cliff, connected to the keep by a staircase inside the chalk. A church was also built inside the cliff, while outside wings, façades, stables, gates were added in the sixteenth and eighteenth centuries. The result is a weird hotchpotch of various styles; walls melt into the rock, windows open into the chalk at unexpected points. The general impression is perhaps intriguing rather than beautiful.

The house is the property of the La Rochefoucauld family, and the Duc wrote some of his maxims here. A century later Hugo, Montalembert and Lamartine were here, also meditating. But despite these associations, despite the unique château, what would draw me back to La Roche Guyon is the place and the setting. The village itself is delightful, full of old houses, lime trees, fountains, inns, squeezed between the cliffs and the river. Above the town, on the road to Gasny, there is a wonderful view over the village at the silver horse-shoe of the river. The distinguished modern novelist Nathalie Sarraute has her country home here. The literary traditions of La Roche Guyon still continue.

From La Roche Guyon you can either take the road that follows the river through Bennecourt and Limetz to Giverny; or you can continue past the view-point, over the hill to Gasny, and then down the pretty Epte valley to Giverny. Or, if you are lucky enough to have friends with a car, you can do both.

In Limetz, however, we ceased for a while to be car-borne. We had got out of the car and wandered into an orchard so that I might photograph the blossom. When we returned, we found that, due to a misunderstanding, we had locked ourselves out of the car. The windows were fastened, the doors were locked, and the only keys were still in the dashboard, tantalizingly out of reach. Hopelessly we tried all the various keys in our pockets, but it was no use.

'We shall have to break a window,' said Hélène Boverat.

Sadly we looked for suitable stones. At this moment another Simca car came down the road, containing three young men. We waved it down and asked if we could try their keys in our door. Helpfully they produced dozens of keys, without any success.

'Let me try,' said a young man with black curly hair.

For the sake of car-owners everywhere I will not describe the next five minutes in detail. But it was instructive to learn how to get into a locked car without breaking anything, with only the aid of a nail-file and a bent nail pulled out of a post. We thanked our Samaritan cordially.

'You are evidently a professional,' I said.

He nodded. 'I have some experience.'

Giverny stands on the Epte at its junction with the Seine. It is another pretty village, but its chief claim to fame is that Monet lived there for forty-three years. After leaving Argenteuil, he settled for a while in Vétheuil, on the bend of the Seine between Rolleboise and La Roche Guyon, until he moved to Giverny in 1883, remaining there, increasingly honoured, until his death. His house, a pleasant shuttered building like a farmhouse, stands back from the road behind a rather dull garden. On the other side of the road, across a small, scarcely-used railway line, is his water garden. It was locked, but we stood on the embankment and peered through the railings.

There, in front of us, were the famous ponds, the Japanese bridge, the much painted water-lilies, the nympheas. The impact was disappointing. It was all so much less watery, so much less lush than I had hoped, although the ponds were large enough and the garden blazed with forsythia and willow green. There were only four lilies where there should be hundreds. Had they died away since his day? The bridge at least was still exactly the same. But then I noticed that someone had since added two central supports. Further thought showed me that the bridge would never have stood without them; Monet had simply left them out of his pictures so that they should not break up his expanse of water and leaves.

Monet's landscapes often strike me as if they had been constructed by a child-snapshotter. He did not always bother to get in the end of the bridge, the side of the portal, the top of the palazzo. But within his arbitrary framework he was not simply a camera. He wanted to transcribe as accurately as possible the interplay of sunlight on colour, light through mist, light on water as it would strike the sensitive eye (or the sensitive film) unfiltered by any preconceived theories about art. But he was quite prepared to leave out the bridge supports or to add some more water-lilies to make his point. And in doing so he brought in his own creative imagination, which raised his canvases from being scientific experiments to works of genius. To revisit the sites of the pictures, where they still exist, is to realize how much extra the Impressionists brought to the innate charm of their subjects. To see the beautiful Seine valley through their eyes is to make it seem even more beautiful; to gild the lily with sunlight and add a few hundred extra for good measure.

The Epte is a small stream by the standards of the other Seine tributaries. Its interest is less economic than scenic and historic. In 911 Rollo, the leader of the Norsemen, met King Charles the Simple ('sincere' would be a better nickname, for he was no fool) of France at St Clair-sur-Epte, who agreed to recognize Norse dominion over the lands north of the Epte, in much the same way as King Alfred the Great had recognized the Danelaw in the North of England. The treaty at St Clair was sealed by the two men shaking hands and by Rollo receiving as a wife Gisèle, the king's daughter. The frontier on the Epte was at first accepted by both sides with good faith, though it later became for hundreds of years a much disputed and blood-stained area.

There are no bloodstains now in that smiling valley. But travelling down the Seine one should not cross the Epte unnoticing. For on the bridge at Giverny we step beyond the Île-de-France on to the mainland, we enter the ancient duchy of Normandy.

6

'Visit Normandy, one of the finest provinces in France, earth of profound history, rich in ancient relics (manor-houses, abbeys, churches), possessing also beaches, resorts, ports, art cities, verdant country, forests and great modern realizations.'

Thus, delightfully, the official hand-out. But in fact the crossing into Normandy is more for the mind's eye, and a romantic, historic one at that, than for the camera. The Seine still pursues its majestic fertile way, the orchards have been with us since Mantes, the forests since Saint-Germain. The ports, abbeys and art cities all still lie ahead. Looking round, I could not see any tall blond blue-eyed Vikings. The people were still small, stocky, Frankish, though many of them seemed to have blue eyes.

But the change was at work, and it was first noticeable in Vernon. Vernon has had more luck than Mantes. Though severely damaged, quite a number of old houses remain. Half-timbered, over-hanging, wonky, I had seen nothing like them on the Seine since Troyes. But these houses, the maisons à pans de bois, as they are called, were carefully preserved or restored, the beams embossed with heads or statuettes. In England, or in Champagne, such houses would be sixteenth century at latest, probably much earlier. But in Normandy the style lingered on and became a matter of region rather than date. A half-timbered Norman house will not usually be as old as a similar building elsewhere. The olde Tudore Forge will be seventeenth or even eighteenth century in Normandy.

Vernon is a pleasant small town. On either side of the river the hills come down fairly steeply to the banks, something which is unique on the Seine and more reminiscent of the Rhine. Both hills are coated with deciduous forests, and the river here is dotted with wooded islands, and the remains of a twelfth-century bridge guarded by a tower. Vernon itself has a fine church with a tall nave and tremendous Romanesque arches – and also, unexpectedly, a splendid rose window, no longer, alas, with stained glass.

I had last been in Vernon twenty-one years earlier, when I had neither the time nor the energy for sightseeing. I had crossed the river on a wet August evening in 1944 by a pontoon bridge called Saul or David or Jonathan or something like that. All day I had stood in the pouring rain in what is now the Avenue Maréchal Montgomery (one of the few signs in France that the whole Liberation was not carried out single-handedly by General Leclerc), counting, checking the vehicles of the Guards Armoured Division as they went down to the bridges, reporting the progress by radio. It was a monotonous occupation, enlivened by only one incident. In the front of one Troop-Carrying Vehicle was an officer with a huge moustache, his head nodding on his chest, fast asleep. The face was familiar. I had seen it contorted with rage over me a couple of years earlier. He had been my platoon officer and instructor, and I had only been a cadet, and my attention had wandered during stalking practice on the heaths round Sandhurst. 'Wake up !' he had screamed at me. 'You're meant to be creeping up on an enemy on the Windsor Ride, not hogging it in bed.' Later he had done a public imitation of me in front of the whole company, and for a while I had feared that my military career was in ruins. And now here he was, far less forgivably, asleep in front of his vehicle as it drove forward into the battle area, while his driver took the wrong fork or drove gaily into an ambush or a minefield. I laughed. We were now the same rank, I would tease him next time we met. But we never met again.

Vernon is not on a bend. Because of the hills on both sides the Seine has to flow fairly straight for a few kilometres. We followed the right bank, through three roadside villages. Happening to stop in Pressagny-l'Orgueilleux, I asked a small dark woman the origin of the name. Why were they proud, again I asked aloud, misquoting Keats, why in the name of glory were they proud? But she did not know and she did not care. The origins, however, of the names of the next two villages, Notre Dame de l'Isle and Port Mort did not need any research.

To the right was the Fprêt de Vernon; its hill flattened out, and the Seine took the opportunity to turn right. Beside us now was the Forêt des Andelys. Ahead were the familiar white cliffs at the next bend. On top of the highest one, white like the cliff itself, was the spectacular ruin of Château Gaillard.

7

Château Gaillard (Saucy Castle, perhaps, or Gallant Castle or Swaggering Castle) was planned in 1196 by King Richard 1 of England, Coeur de Lion, to protect his Norman Duchy against the attacks of the Franks. He drove his engineers and builders hard, despite the obstruction of the Archbishop of Rouen, and after a year he was able to exclaim: 'How beautiful she is, my year-old daughter'.

Richard had studied fortress architecture not only in Europe but also in the Holy Land; and Château Gaillard was undoubtedly a masterpiece. It was constructed on a complicated plan: a keep within a fort within a moat within a court within huge outer walls within another moat. Alone on its height it was connected with the rest of the plateau by a small ridge defended by a separate fort, the Châtelet. Richard's engineers diverted a tributary of the Seine to isolate the foot of the cliff too, to form yet another moat. A well was driven down through the chalk to the fresh water at the foot. Château Gaillard was impregnable, the greatest fort in Europe, the rock which dominated and guarded the approaches to Normandy.

King Philippe Auguste of France was not pleased. 'If its walls were made of solid iron,' he cried, 'yet would I take them.'

Richard answered, 'By the throat of God, if its walls were made of butter, yet would I hold them'.

This amiable dialogue between the two Crusader Kings was, it is said, screamed across the ramparts. But I cannot visualize the scene. Even assuming that Philippe Auguste was willing to come within arrow-shot of the walls, such complicated conditional sentences would have been lost on the breeze and the two kings would have been left shouting, 'Comment? Je n'entends pas' at each other. Perhaps the conversation really took place through a messenger.

The castle became the seat of Richard's small court and it was there that he worked out the political strategy aimed at encircling the Franks, a plan which Richard's death at Chalus brought to nothing. But under the vacillating King John things were very different. Philippe Auguste, crossing Normandy, capturing castle after castle, found himself before the Saucy Castle itself and decided to besiege it. His preparations were careful and elaborate; he attacked the villages of Les Andelys at the foot, driving twelve hundred old men, women and children to take refuge in the castle, to be bouches inutiles. Then he closed his lines round the castle with a double ditch and wooden towers. The defending commander, the Connetable de Lascy, worried about his food reserves, drove out the bouches inutiles, but Philippe Auguste refused to let them pass his lines and they had to remain where the sunken road now is, between the walls and the besiegers. They stayed there without food or shelter through a long cold winter under the eyes of both sides, reduced to the final horror of cannibalism.

However, in March 1204, finding the siege too slow, Philippe Auguste decided to assault the castle. He first undermined the Châtelet, forcing the English to abandon it. Then some men climbed into the courtyard through the latrines and let down the drawbridge. The French swarmed in, broke down the main gate with a battering ram and took the garrison prisoner before they had time to retreat into the keep. It was all really very simple, and Philippe Auguste was so pleased that he allowed the defenders to remain unchained. Shortly afterwards he captured Rouen and the rest of Normandy.

A hundred years later a distressing episode took place at Château Gaillard. King Louis x accused his wife, Marguerite de Bourgogne, of adultery and debauchery and imprisoned her there, together with her sister. They were kept in a lightless dungeon, their only daylight being a brief escorted visit each day to the chapel. After two years Marguerite was strangled and her sister ordered to a convent. But the sister resisted and remained in the dungeon for another five years. When she was finally carried into the convent, she was insane.

During the Hundred Years' War, Château Gaillard changed hands many times. Henry v besieged it successfully in 1418. The following year the French under La Hire recaptured it by assault. The following year the English were back again. And so it continued. The same thing happened during the Wars of Religion. Indeed, the remarkable thing about the impregnable castle was how often it was successfully captured. Not once did it succeed in resisting assault or siege. Perhaps it was not such a military masterpiece after all.

It was finally destroyed by order of Henri iv, who thought it a risk in his turbulent kingdom. Now it is only a white ruin cared for by the Beaux Arts. Grass and wildflowers cover the site of so much heroism and misery and the view is glorious. To our right was the village of Petit Andely; at our feet was the Seine, a curve of liquid pewter, with its white cliffs, its island, its surface rippled by the barges. Beyond to the far distance were the woods and the fields and the hills of Normandy. A fresh April wind blew in our faces, shadows chased each other across the plateau behind us, the grass was springy under our feet. But remembering the bouches inutiles, remembering Queen Marguerite and her sister, Château Gaillard is a place to take away your appetite; which is a pity, considering the excellent restaurants in Les Andelys.

8

I was back in Les Andelys at the end of July. The freshness had gone from the breeze, the greenness from the fields. It was hot summer and the corn stooks were piled on the stubble. This time I gave only the briefest glance to Château Gaillard framed by the village street like Mont Blanc. I looked longer at the fair in the village square, and then I went in to the 'Chaine d'Or' for dinner.

The 'Chaine d'Or' (from the former chain across the river for toll collecting) is an eighteenth-century inn built round a court-yard beside the river. Its dining-room was timbered and the old hearth smelt of wood smoke. My table was beside the window, beside the summer evening river. Before me were the details of the menu touristique, the menu gastronomique, the carte.

Gone were the days of steak and chips. I was back in the world of butter and cream and huge portions; it was like being in Burgundy again. Moules à la crême, escalope à la crême, poularde à la crême, sole à la crême – I ate them all in my first forty-eight hours at the 'Chaine d'Or'. So that I might continue to eat like that after I returned home, I was given the recipe.

You take your veal (or chicken or sole or what have you) and fry it in plenty of Normandy butter. Then you sprinkle it freely with calvados and flambé it. When the flickering blue flames have gone out, you take the veal out and put it somewhere warm. Then to the mixture of butter and burnt calvados you add lots of thick Norman cream and mushrooms (but no flour), cook till it is hot and pour it on the veal. To make a variation you can call it Sauce Normande or Sauce Vallée d'Auge or, if it is a fish dish, you can add mussels or shrimps.

This information, which does not agree with Michelin's des-cription, was given me by a neighbour, a bulky, friendly man. 'You can put Sauce Normande on anything,' he told me, 'chicken, veal, fish, eggs, vegetables, game. Anything. You can eat it every day.'

'It's delicious,' I said, 'but a little rich, don't you think?' After only twenty-four hours I was already beginning to wilt.

'To make the sauce richer,' he went on, 'you can add the yolks of two or three eggs, if you like.'

'Yes, I suppose you could.'

'Before the war we used to make the sauce richer by adding blood. A woman would come round all the houses early each morning calling "Sang! Sang!" and we would buy a litre or a half-litre each. But they do not sell blood like that any more.'

'How sad!'

He patted his large stomach affectionately. 'Les Normands sont très gourmands.'

After dinner I sat on the terrace and looked at the dark river and the fluted wakes of the barges where they caught the lights. I drank calvados, vieux calvados.

I had been told by the café proprietor across the square that there were three kinds of calvados: calvados ordinaire or vert, mainly used by labourers for lacing their breakfast coffee, bon calvados, and vieux calvados. I tried all three. The ordinaire, which I sampled a little later in the day than the time recommended, was sharp, clean, tasting strongly of apples. The bon was smoother and the taste of apples, though distinctive, was less noticeable. The vieux calvados came in bottles with long necks and artificially old labels, and it hardly tasted at all of apples.

'Vieux calvados is very like cognac,' I remarked to my Norman friend.

He would have none of it. 'One could perhaps say that cognac tastes like vieux calvados.'

But Petit Andely has more to offer than the pleasures of the table. It is a delightful village full of half-timbered houses, the beam-ends carved with small statues, the roofs steep and tiled. On one roof I noticed that someone had fixed models of a cat and a rat. I knocked at the door and asked Madame the purpose of these objects.

'Pour s'amuser,' she said.

I mentioned that in England it had often been the custom in earlier times to bury a mummified cat and rat in the thatch for luck.

'Ah bon?' she said.

Petit Andely has a pleasant twelfth-century church in the square, in the shape of a Greek cross. Inside, slender columns, bulging ominously, soar to great vaults. In the porch is a statue of Saint Sauveur to which the faithful had attached bunches of grapes and ribbons. As a change from old buildings there are always the curving banks of the Seine, the tireless fishermen, the white cliffs on either side, the endless procession of barges. I found Petit Andely enchanting.

Grand Andely is half a mile inland and much less charming.

It has been extensively rebuilt and the banks, schools and shops are large, modern and unenticing. The sixteenth-century church, however, remains and contains some fine Renaissance windows illustrating distressing executions. But I was on the trail of another water-goddess, and I made the pilgrimage to the fountain of Sainte-Clotilde.

Sainte Clotilde was a far from legendary person. She was the wife of Clovis, King of the Franks, and her miracle was in changing water into wine for the benefit of thirsty labourers who were building a convent. Her fountain is a small pool like a wishing-well in the corner of a walled garden. It only contains water, clear water and a silver bottom covered with coins thrown in by the hopeful. Above it is an old lime tree that has been there for six hundred years or more, its great branches now supported by crutches, but still in full vigorous leaf.

Across the road is one of the few remaining old houses in Grand Andely, the birthplace and childhood home of Poussin. In the middle of the Monet country it was startling to find the most severe of classical painters, and perhaps salutary to recall that there have been other schools of painting than the Impressionists, other artistic objectives than the exact rendering of light effects. Form, construction, drawing rather than colour were Poussin's guides and it would have been unthinkable to him to paint anything other than scenes from the Bible, from Roman history or classical mythology. When we look at his canvases in Paris or London (or in Grand Andely which owns his 'Coriolanus') we move away from the Seine valley and the Norman light. We are back in a landscape of super-Dolomites and feathery trees and the inhabitants are usually naked and capering.

The odd thing is that Poussin's theoretical aims were not so far from Monet's. Fidelity to Nature was all-important to him, its shapes and proportions provided the order his art required. He would collect stones and grasses and study them with the same care that Monet studied water. But the results of his passion for accuracy are surprising. Looking at Poussin's pictures one would never guess that he had ever seen a real mountain or tree or cloud any more than a Bacchanal.

9

I left Les Andelys by bus, my old favourite form of transport, and the road ran between the cliffs and the river. Then the cliffs died away, the valley flattened and the river prepared to turn again. At this moment we suddenly crossed the river by a large concrete suspension bridge. This was so unexpected in that pastoral landscape that I got off the bus for a closer look.

It was, I discovered, not really built of concrete. The girders and wire ropes were merely cased in wood which was then coated in cement for protection. The effect was bizarre. Suspension bridges are big bold mobiles of steel and grace and air. Concrete bridges are solid and strong and earthy. To find the two mingled was disturbing, like finding a glass steamroller or an aircraft built of Portland stone.

However, it was a record span for a bridge of that type and it had been opened by M. Mendès-France in 1947. The other half of the bridge – an island divides them – was an ordinary low barge-hindering bridge and it had been opened in 1942 by M. Jacques Boulloche, the Inspector General of Bridges and Roads, just before his deportation to Buchenwald where he died.

I found myself in the village of Saint-Pierre-de-Vauvray. It was, alas, the first charmless village I had seen since before Mantes; no tiled roofs, no timbered walls, no old inns, just a railway station, and some station cafés and a concrete hotel related to the bridge. It seemed a sad come-down after Petit Andely. However, I soon found ample compensations. My bedroom window looked on to an orchard where the apples were starting to blush. There was a line of poplars beyond, and the Seine sliding by. And there was Passetoutgrain for dinner at five francs a bottle.

Passetoutgrain! That unforgettable name took me straight back to Burgundy and the petite Seine, that trickling bubbling stream you could jump across. I ordered a bottle.

It came, the filthiest bottle I have ever seen, black with soot and cobwebs. Where did the hotel keep its wine, I wondered, in a chimney? It made black marks on the table-cloth; the waitress apologized and tried to clean the bottle, but I stopped her. Gingerly I scraped the label clean with the corner of an envelope. The date was 1952.

I do not know if many other people in the world have drunk thirteen-year-old Passetoutgrain. Such a modest wine is normally drunk a year old; this must have lain forgotten and ignored all that time. Sacrificing my handkerchief I wrapped it round the neck and poured out. It was delicious. Clear, smooth, subtle. Nutty? No, more complicated than that. Burnt? No, not really a burnt taste. Smoky? Not in the ordinary meaning of the word. Extraordinary. I poured out a second glass.

Madame came up smiling. 'I see you are enjoying my little wine.' Mon petit vin.

I said it was delicious. But it was unusual to find Passetoutgrain so old.

She said, 'I am fortunate, I have a large cellar, I can keep my wine a long time. And I still sell it at the 1952 price.'

My example, I noticed, was being followed. The rest of the dining-room were keeping up with Jones and the dirty bottles were sprouting on every table like toadstools. The waitress looked harassed.

I had intended to leave Saint-Pierre by the first bus the following morning, but now there seemed to be no reason to hurry. So I wandered by the Seine looking at the fishermen. There were dozens of them, in punts moored to poles, between the islands or in the channel obstructed by the late M. Boulloche's bridge. Then I went back to the hotel for roast chicken and more Passetoutgrain. We were down to half-bottles now, which caused twice as much mess and reduced the waitress to despair. When I left Saint-Pierre there was no more Passetoutgrain in that cellar.

The road still followed the Seine and the feeling of the countryside was very English; rolling country, stubble fields, downs, pasture with brown Norman cows, brindled cows, even white cows. The villages were pretty with flint or brick walls and roofs of old tile or thatch. Take away a few poplars, add some oaks and a hedge or two, and I might have been in Hampshire.

At Connelles my attention was awakened by a long wall, its top thatched and planted with irises. It must look amazing in spring-time. The temptation was completed by the sight of the 'Auberge du Coin Rêvé'. I seized my bag and leapt off the bus.

The 'Auberge du Coin Rêvé' – what a name! – does not face the Seine, but it is a pretty inn with a chestnut-shaded garden. I sat there and ordered a glass of cider. It seemed an appropriate drink.

'We do not serve glasses of cider,' said the girl. 'Only cidre bouché, bottled cider.'

I ordered a bottle. It came, unassuming and unlabelled, bottled if not in the auberge itself at least nearby. The cork was held down by rusty wire. The cider was brown, slightly sweet, fizzing, with a light sediment. It was neither pleasing nor displeasing and I felt no urge to pour out a second glass.

'Do you sell much cider?' I asked the girl.

'Un peu.' She suddenly smiled. 'Très peu.'

'In England we drink quite a lot of cider,' I remarked.

'You have cider in England too?' she asked unbelievingly, and left me alone under the chestnut leaves.

Later I discovered she was quite right. I was the only person I ever saw in Normandy drinking cider. What on earth do they do with all those apples, I wonder. Does it all go in calvados and tarte aux pommes? Or is there some industrial use for the product?

Beyond Connelles the cliffs were back beside the road, hanging above us, the edges often broken off into lone sentinels of chalk, like giant statues of saints staring across the valley. At Amfreville-sous-les-Monts I hopped off the bus again. The 'Café de Passage' offered food at any time, and I was hungry.

I was served a large meal by Catherine, the daughter of the house, a soft-voiced girl in white jeans. She was a type I had not seen before, slim, snub-nosed with a helmet of blonde hair; the first Norman I had seen in Normandy. 'Could I have a glass of cider?' I asked.

'We have only bottles, m'sieu,' she whispered. It was a wasteful way to drink, to order a large bottle and only drink one glass. But

I did it all the same. The cider was just the same as the other. On the other side of the room were four men playing cards, all drinking red wine. One licked his fingers carefully each time before touching a card and they all hurled down their cards on to the table with the full strength of their shoulders. Their voices and laughter were deafening, and I do not suppose that Catherine ever made herself heard in that establishment. I ventured to interrupt, to ask the way to the locks and to the Côte des Deux Amants. One of them came to the door to show me the way.

'Take care on the Côte des Deux Amants!' he advised. 'It is very steep.' He patted his heart ominously.

I left my suitcase in Catherine's care and walked along the river bank. The Seine, so wide, thick, brown, glassy, was being cut into curves by a water-skier. I did not envy him the moment when he would finally let go the rope and sink into that polluted water. Across the river was the pleasant water-front of Poses, pastel coloured, tree lined, straggling along the bank. Poses is, like Saint-Pierre-de-Vauvray, a great centre of fishing; indeed, every café in those parts carries notices about the Association de Pêche or the Amis Pêcheurs.

Joining Amfreville-sous-les-Monts and Poses are the great locks and the huge weir. Both are remarkable engineering achievements; the big lock is over seven hundred feet long and is worked entirely by electricity. A British ship, the *Somme*, was passing through as I watched; it didn't seem to take very long. Another ship, the *Garonne*, was waiting to come downstream on its way to Dundee. A barge was in a smaller lock; the bargee's wife had been shopping at the lock shop and now stood placidly beside me waiting for the lock to fill.

Were there many British ships passing through, I asked her.

'Many.'

And what did they usually carry?

She shrugged. 'Everything. Tractors, machinery, cheese, wine, everything.'

The Poses weir is amazing. It is adjustable, the control point of the Seine, where the flow of the river, such as it is, can be increased or retarded. Above the weir the Seine is still glassy, immobile, untroubled by thoughts of the cataclysm just ahead. Fish in their hundred flicker along the rim a few inches from disaster. And then over the edge, a khaki Niagara, a swirling, boiling torrent foaming with detergents and chemical effluents. It is an abrupt and astonishing change to come over the stately river, something totally out of character. And the Seine is never the same again, for below Poses the river is tidal; it flows strongly upstream or downstream, no longer its own master, controlled by the movements of a sea still eighty miles away.

10

At Poses the Seine is joined by the Andelle, a small fast-flowing river; and above the junction there is a steep grassy hill, the Côte des Deux Amants. Several writers, including in the twelfth century Marie de France, the first French woman novelist, have given versions of the romance of the Deux Amants, which may be summarized as follows:

Once upon a time there lived a wicked baron called Rulph and he had a sweet daughter called Calixte, who was much admired for her beauty and fatness. Rulph was unwilling to part with his daughter and her dowry, and all her suitors were required to carry her up the hill without pausing for a moment. Many suitors tried but they all abandoned the test halfway and Calixte grew weary of being dumped on the hillside. Her heart was given to a young esquire called Raoul (or in some versions Edmond), who, not even being a knight, was even less approved of than the others. However, he was allowed to try. All the inhabitants from the nearby villages and castles came to watch as he took Calixte on his back and began the climb. His snorts and pants could be heard for miles, but he struggled on. He reached the summit without pausing, grasped the flagstaff – and fell dead. Calixte's reactions are variously described: she dropped dead at his side; she picked up his body and embracing it jumped over the edge to certain death; she went into a convent; she grew so thin pining for Raoul that the next suitor had no trouble in carrying her up, and she married him and lived happily ever after.

Now, climbing the Côte des Deux Amants I wondered what all the fuss was about. By the way everyone went on you would think it was the Matterhorn. The hill is neither very steep nor very high; modern infantrymen climb far longer and worse cliffs in Christmas-tree order with full packs and mortars and what-have-you without having heart attacks. I flatter myself that in my prime I could have won Calixte without killing myself. Indeed, I pondered going back to the café and borrowing Catherine for the afternoon, but she was no doubt busy and my motives might be misunderstood and anyway she was very slim. Calixte must indeed have been heavy, or Raoul dreadfully unfit; or both.

In which case, I mused as I plodded upwards without pausing, he should have fallen back on cunning, that quality so much admired in the Middle Ages. He should have postponed the test day after day by various ruses, while he trained furiously with a rucksack full of stones and Calixte dieted. And then –

But I had reached the top of the hill, and my mind was distracted by a marvellous panorama. Below me was the Seine, glassy or swirling; there were the islands, ships, water-skiers, barges, fishermen in their punts. Beyond was the Norman countryside, woods, orchards, harvest fields. To my left were the chalk cliffs with their dramatic sentinels. To my right, over the hill, was the sky smudged by the factories of Rouen.

I wandered down the hill. In a house beside the road a wedding reception was being held. Encore deux amants, I thought, glancing in. The bride was small and stocky, the groom seemed a hefty young man. He would have little difficulty in carrying her wherever he liked. Back at the 'Café de Passage' the four men were still hurling down their no doubt by now very sticky cards. I waved at them and collected my suitcase from Catherine.

'I climbed the Côte des Deux Amants,' I said, 'and, voilà, I am still alive.'

'Ah bon?' she whispered.

When my bus came the driver welcomed me as an old friend. One of the bewildering things about this journey was that no matter where and when I caught this bus, it was always the same driver.

'You are a good client,' he said.

'I am practically en pension,' I answered. 'Will you be taking me right to the sea?'

'Alas no, monsieur. Only as far as Rouen.'

11

I came into Rouen by the right way, along the Corniche, and my first sight of the city was the famous view from the hill, facing the setting sun. All the way from Saint-Pierre-de-Vauvray I had had the strange feeling that I was driving through England, and the feeling had increased as we approached the city. To stand on the top of Saint Catherine's Hill, overlooking the city surrounded by chalk downs, is to wonder if you are looking at Rouen or Winchester. Before you lie the old Roman camp, the Norman capital, the medieval market-town with its timbered houses, the vast cathedral. William the Conqueror must often have felt pangs of doubt about which city he was in at the moment.

The analogy, however, should not be pressed too far. Nothing could be further from the squat tower of Winchester Cathedral than the spire of Rouen, the tallest in France, almost five hundred feet high. And there is an even greater contrast between the two rivers, the little bubbling trout-filled Itchen and the great Seine, its banks lined with wharves and sea-going ships. It is these two features that dominate the view from the Côte Sainte Catherine; the cathedral with its towers and the river catching the light, shining like metal. Round the cathedral were the spires and towers of the other churches, and on the left bank was a shapely modern skyscraper housing the Norman archives. The Seine was frilly with a hundred and six cranes. It was a poetic moment.

I had come to Rouen with an introduction from a friend to Monsieur Robert Toussaint of the Union Maritime. I called at his office and in no time we were seated in an old restaurant in the

Place du Vieux Marché, separated only by an enormous quantity of food and wine. Outside in the square was the tablet marking the place where Joan of Arc was burnt, a sobering sight for lunchtime revels. The restaurant itself was half-timbered, and very old (though restored since the war); no doubt some of the thirsty crowd came in here to refresh themselves after a burning.

Flames were in our minds now as we talked. Monsieur Toussaint and a friend, Monsieur Nicole, who had joined us for lunch, told me about the semaine rouge, the terrible week in March 1944 when the allies had bombed the bridges every morning at eleven o'clock. All the bridges had been destroyed, though one, the railway bridge, had required a 'suicide raid' by a British fighter-bomber to bring it down. The damage to Rouen itself had been very great, though the real conflagration, I was told, had been four years earlier. After the French campaign was over the Germans set fire to the old quarter of Rouen, for no very obvious reason except amusement; the narrow winding streets, the old half-timbered houses were soon burning merrily and the Rouen fire brigades were ordered not to interfere on pain of being shot. The area on the right bank between the river and the cathedral was left a blackened wilderness.

Old Rouen was, of course, irreplaceable, but for industrial Rouen it was something of a blessing, heavily disguised. The nineteenth-century industrialization had hit Rouen everywhere. Much of the city, and in particular the left bank, was a formless jumble of factories, warehouses, docks, sidings. After the war the opportunity was taken to replan all this, to move the factories further out, to turn the left bank into a residential area, to allow the city for the first time to spread along both banks. The Rouennais have always looked on the Seine rather as something on the edge of the city where ships were unloaded. The idea of using it for pleasure is something new. The island of Lacroix is gradually being cleared of its warehouses and factories and replanted with gardens and sports grounds.

All this was told me by Monsieur Nicole, who was on the Municipal Council and involved with these matters. 'But it is easier said than done,' he remarked wryly. 'There are many problems, many interests involved.'

We had by now reached the coffee-and-old-calvados stage and I thanked them both for giving me so much of their time, and Monsieur Toussaint for his lavish hospitality.

He said, 'We have a phrase in Normandy: "The friend of a friend is my friend".'

This charming sentence was, it seemed, capable of geometric expansion. I rapidly began to acquire new friends at an increasing rate. Apart from Monsieur Nicole, I was soon introduced to the Chief Engineer of the Port of Rouen, and to Monsieur René Herval, ex-president of the Academy of Rouen and President of the Society of Norman Writers. Between them all they covered almost every aspect of Rouen life that might interest me; we were lacking, it seemed to me, only the Chief of Police and the Archbishop.

I said to Monsieur Herval, 'Tell me, monsieur, just what does the Seine mean to you?'

He stared at me, his eyes widened, he spoke. I wish I had space here to reproduce the high eloquence of his answer, his vision of the Seine as a channel of civilization and commerce and culture.

'Would you say,' I went on, 'that the Seine's unique quality lay in being at the same time a channel of communication and a frontier?'

He would not agree at all. The Seine had only been a frontier in pre-Roman times, when it was the boundary between the Belgae and the Armoricae, and then it had not been a channel of communication.

This erudite dialogue took place in the Chief Engineer's office overlooking the port. The engineer himself was trying to give me charts of the bed of the Seine and tonnages of exports and imports. Monsieur Nicole was trying to tell me about the new municipal buildings across the river. Monsieur Toussaint was on the telephone to his office to get a car and a driver for me. Secretaries brought me coffee. I had an awful feeling that I was bringing the Port of Rouen to a halt.

Later, driving in Monsieur Toussaint's car with Monsieur

Herval beside me, I toured the panoramas of Rouen; from the terrace at Canteleu, from the new university on the Mont Saint-Aignan (how this saint keeps cropping up on the Seine! In fact his great feat was on the Loire, defending Orléans against the Huns) and above all from the Côte Sainte Catherine. From some angles the city was dominated by the churches, from others by the port, from others again by the factories. And always there were the hills with their chalk cliffs and beech woods, and the river cleaving the city like a scimitar.

The Romans called it Rotomagus, Monsieur Herval explained. It was the lowest point on the Seine where a bridge could be built; their bridge crossed the river at the island. And the hills round, they sheltered it like a cradle. 'Paris is rather like it,' he added Norman-fashion.

I mentioned what an improvement it was moving the factories farther out.

'Not far enough,' he growled. 'In winter, when it rains and the clouds are low, the city smells,' he said, lapsing from his lofty eloquence, 'like cats' piss.'

I could not impose on my friends all the time, and I spent my days wandering about the streets by myself. I was happy to find that, despite the war, a great deal of Old Rouen does still survive. To wander down little narrow streets like the rue Damiette or the rue des Fosses Louis VIII or the Impasse des Hauts-Mariages is to be once again in a medieval town of half-timbered houses, all preserved or restored with a care which would astonish the citizens of Troyes if they should ever come. For Rouen is prosperous and is very much aware of the treasure in its midst. At the end of almost every street is a church tower or spire, like Troyes, but it is an improvement to find that the street itself is not falling down.

My favourite street, like everyone else's, is the rue du Gros Horloge. A busy crowd of shoppers moves up and down it; at one end is the enormous cathedral, at the other end the Vieux Marché, and in the middle, straddling the street, is the great clock, so beloved by the Rouennais. A single hand, with a lamb on the end, moves round the big golden face telling the time quite accurately, it seemed to me. An aperture also gives the phases of the moon, in case you might need to know them. Beside the clock is the old belfry and, built into its base, is an incongruous but charming eighteenth-century fountain, put there by the Duc de Montmorency as a symbol of his happiness.

The Norman capital, as might be expected, is noted for its food. I had already eaten moules marinières and tripes au calvados under the eye of Monsieur Toussaint. Now I went to 'Le Beffroi' for further research. It is a fourteenth-century house, a maze of twisting staircases and black beams, and rather uncomfortably recalls the time when Joan of Arc was in the nearby dungeon. Inside are some alarming silver presses for crushing carcases. Thumbscrews, dungeons, belfries – it all seemed uncompromisingly medieval.

I ordered of course caneton à la Rouennais, the famous Norman dish, perhaps the most formidable of French dishes. You first take your duckling and strangle it (offstage) so that none of the precious blood may be lost in the killing. Then you roast it lightly, cutting off the legs and wings and grilling them separately. Then you show the carcase to the hungry guest to encourage him. You carve the duck into slices, put them on a silver platter, sprinkle them with pepper, pour on brandy and set fire to it. When the flames are out, you pour over everything a special thick sauce made from the carcase crushed in one of the silver thumbscrews. I am not perfectly clear about the contents of the sauce – the master chef deals with this personally – but I gathered it was mainly composed of mousse de foie gras and blood. The result is amazing, unforgettable, the final spire on the tower of Norman cooking. But it is not a dish to be ordered lightly and especially not by those in a hurry or in trouble with their livers or bank manager.

Afterwards I walked it off through the streets of Rouen. I was feeling medieval too. The Earl of Warwick was captain of Rouen and Joan was still involved in the long theological argument with her French judges. The narrow streets were full of shadows; some were so narrow that they were almost tunnels. And always at the end of the street was a floodlit tower or spire, like a stone flame against the black sky.

Rouen goes to bed late for a provincial city. At midnight the bars and cafés were still full of gay, rather noisy young people.

The difference between Troyes and Rouen was noticeable at night too; here the teenagers seemed to have more vitality, more joie de vivre, more money; they were better dressed, less bored. In a men's clothes shop in the rue de la République I noticed a garment displayed, which was described as 'Le New Standing James Bond, élégant, sobre et sportif'. It was, alas, only a drab, fawn raincoat which Bond himself would never have worn, even under torture, but at least it showed a certain measure of sophistication.

I went into a nearby bar, and ordered a glass of vieux calvados. I watched the people, wondering who they were. Who were these well-dressed unattached women and what were they doing in a bar at midnight? Was I in a rendezvous for more successful prostitutes? But no one accosted me, no one came to sit at my table. I got up and slipped through the door marked 'Toilettes Téléphone'. There was no toilet, no telephone, only a staircase leading to an upper floor guarded by a large growling Alsatian dog. The patronne followed me and hauled me back. 'You must not go in there, monsieur,' she said firmly, leading me back to my table.

My eye was taken by a woman, a platinum blonde in a tight mauve suit. She was vivacious and seemed to know everyone. She had a deep voice and big hands and kissed everyone, men and women alike, with lasciviousness. I shrank back behind my calvados and tried not to catch her eye. Had I wandered into a lesbians' bar, I wondered. Further surreptitious examination, however, convinced me that she really was a man. Both men and women greeted him alike with the same 'Bonsoir, ça va? Ugh! Ne me touchez pas!', but nobody asked him to leave.

Those ruthless Rouen novelists, Flaubert, Maupassant, Gide, might have found material in it, I reflected, but in my medieval mood, my mind full of Bishop Cauchon and the Earl of Warwick, it seemed out of key. And then I remembered that something in the same vein had happened here before. For was not transvestism the ultimately unforgivable crime of Joan of Arc, the one for which she was sent to the stake?

The following morning I went again to the Vieux Marché. A flagstone marks the site of the stake and someone had placed a sheaf of gladioli on it. Poor young Joan, I thought, so alone in her fearful ordeal; the English, the French, the Burgundians all against her, all wanting her dead. A new theory, however, is that she was not executed at all. She was smuggled away the night before and someone else was induced to take her place. Who that someone was and what the inducement is not clear, but I felt that she too deserved flowers.

The Vieux Marché is still an active market, full of jostling shoppers and men carrying crates, full of fruit and fish and cheeses. I paused admiringly before the cheeses. Since entering Normandy I had been once again in great cheese country. Meal after meal, having, I felt, eaten enough to last me the rest of my life, my eye would fall on the cheese-board covered in soft ripe cheeses, and I would be tempted and succumb. The two strongest are the longest established; both Pont l'Evêque and Livarot date from the thirteenth century, Pont l'Evêque square and brown and creamy with an enticing taste of drying thatch, Livarot in cylindrical shape, paler, with a bewitching odour of dung. Port Salut is mild and soft with a thick rind, but it is now often made in factories and stamped with trade names and slogans. And, of course, Camembert.

Camembert is a relative newcomer among Norman cheeses. It was invented in the nineteenth century by a farm woman called Marie Harel, and she should, if her rights were properly protected, have become a millionairess. With the possible exception of Canadian Cheddar, it must be the most eaten cheese in the world. Too often nowadays it is made in a factory outside Normandy and left to ripen in its box during its unpredictable journey from factory to shop. So many Camemberts even in France are chalky and salt or brown and ammoniac; in Normandy where they care for their cheeses it is usually better, and Camembert at its best can be very good indeed. But judged by the highest standards, compared with Brie or Coulommiers, I find it unsubtle.

However, I have been on occasion delighted to meet it. In 1944 we arrived in Normandy expecting to find the local population, those that had not fled, near starving. We spent some days in reserve, camped by an undamaged farm near Bayeux, which promptly put up a sign 'Oeufs, Beurre, Fromage'. Accustomed to wartime shortages we hourly expected the sign to be changed to 'No eggs, butter, cheese'. But it never was. Our farmer had a continent's supply of Camembert in his store-house and he was only too keen to sell them to us. What a marvellous taste that Camembert had! After years of wartime ration cheese I had almost forgotten what cheese could be like. We ate Camembert for breakfast, lunch, tea and supper. With it we ate, not fresh crusty French bread, but army biscuits, and we drank with it, not, as the French recommend, a Vougeot, a Beaune or a Haut-Brion, but sweet army compo tea. It is perhaps in retaliation for this that the French now recommend tea as the only possible drink to accompany Caerphilly.

Now, surveying the groaning cheese-stalls in the Vieux Marché I found one I did not know: Boursin. There were apparently two versions, Boursin a l'Ail and Boursin au Poivre. I bought them both. Yes, indeed, Madame assured me, I would find them delicious. Look what it said on the label, seventy-five per cent fat matter! And the others had only forty-five or fifty per cent! They were in fact fairly ordinary cream cheeses, one tasting, as might be expected, of garlic, the other of pepper.

From cheese to wine, from mountains of Camembert to gallons of wine. Rouen has wine stores capable of holding 180,000 hecto-litres at one time, and one was the largest single store in Europe. I was shown round it by the manager.

It was a marvellous sight for anyone who appreciates gargantua, the awareness of plenty: a modern vase of Vix. It was, however, nothing to give pleasure to those who worry about whether their wine is château-bottled or whether it has been shipped in oak-casks, which may or may not slightly affect the taste. This wine arrived from North Africa in tankers and was pumped directly to the stores by underground pipelines.

The manager showed me the whole process. I apologized for taking his time, but he brushed it away. The wine entered here through these valves, this pump, those pipes. It was stored in these tanks. It passed through those pumps to that loading bay, and it was loaded through hoses into tanker-lorries to be driven away and blended into vin ordinaire or transformed magically into Beaujolais or Côtes du Rhône.

Inside it was a mass of pipes and valves and pumps and electric dials. Only the pervading smell of wine showed that we were not in an oil refinery. In the concrete floor beneath us were large trap-doors opening into underground tanks, oubliettes where one might fall and drown and be forgotten for ever – only they were empty.

'But where is the wine?' I asked.

Up iron ladders were more tanks, more dials, overalled work-men. The manager was telling me about so many hectolitres an hour, so many kilograms per square centimetre, which red lights went on automatically to show which tank was running dry.

'But where is the wine?' I asked.

Gradually the horrid truth dawned. There was no wine. The whole place was empty, as empty as the vase of Vix.

Yes, alas, the manager admitted, there had been no imports of wine for a long time. For over a year. He did not know why. Some said it was because of a political embargo; others said it was because the Algerians had forgotten how to make wine now that the French had left. He hoped there might be some wine this autumn, but he did not know.

I thanked him again for showing me round, but I did not apologize again for taking up his time. I must have been the bright spot of his day.

Apart from wine, Rouen is a thriving port, the third port of France and the first river port, ahead of Bordeaux and Nantes. Before the war it was the principal port for coal imports from Britain, but now that that trade has died, it is principally occupied with vegetables, fruit (in particular bananas), cereals, machinery and general cargoes. Much of its trade is with the Mediterranean countries and it is a striking example of the cheapness of sea trans-port, as against rail, that importers should prefer to bring in their Mediterranean vegetables through Rouen and not through Marseilles. As I walked along the wharves I noticed a Greek ship unloading; and Greece is a long way from Rouen by sea.

Rouen's great advantage lies in its nearness to Paris and the great centres of production and consumption in the Paris area. It is in fact the nearest port to Paris.

'I suppose,' I remarked to Monsieur Toussaint, 'that every ship that docks here is one taken from Le Havre.'

His eyes twinkled. 'What makes you say that?' he asked.

In fact there is considerable rivalry between the two Seine ports. Rouen is very conscious of its advantages. It has modern facilities, a sufficient labour force available; and the extra hundred kilometres on the voyage, six hours' sailing, is in fact an advantage as it is all a movement in the right direction. The Rouennais look forward to the time when all cargoes will be handled in Rouen, leaving Le Havre to handle only the ferries and the transatlantic liners. The Havrais, I was later to find, do not see it this way at all. Monsieur Toussaint, a Havrais living in Rouen, was carefully impartial.

All the same, Rouen has had a considerable technical problem: the opening of the port to ships of greater draught. The deepening of the river itself was not a very difficult task. The river-bottom was water-resisting, and only normal dredging was required on a channel 150 to 200 yards wide. But the deepening of the Seine estuary channel was much tougher. The conditions there were very difficult; enormous quantities of fine sand washed about the bay, the currents were more than five knots and the spring tides reached more than twenty-five feet. Over five million cubic metres of sand were dredged out of the channel every year, but it soon washed back, and only ships drawing less than eighteen feet at neap-tide or twenty-five feet at high tide could get up to Rouen.

Finally the Port of Rouen decided that there was nothing for it but to move the navigable channel in the estuary. It can be imagined what a gigantic task this was. Scale models were made and studied by the Laboratoire Sogreah of Grenoble, experts played happily with sand and water and artificial currents, and a new channel was chosen which would make the tide the friend of Rouen and not the enemy. It was opened in the autumn of 1959 after more than ten years' work. The new course had been dug in sandbanks, and involved shifting over fifty million cubic feet of sand; about six miles of dikes had been demolished, twenty miles of new dikes built, all in the most difficult conditions, all without disturbing shipping. Now the tide and the currents started to work for the channel instead of against it; instead of silting up the new route the tide began in 1961 to scour it out, deepening it naturally by about three feet every year. By 1964 the new channel was some ten feet deeper than the old and Rouen was accessible to ships drawing twenty-five feet at any tide.

I could not help saluting such ingenious and patient work and I hoped that the port of Rouen would reap comparable benefits from this expense. Certainly there seemed to be plenty of ships in the port, not only Mediterranean, but from Britain, Scandinavia and Germany. One of them, I noticed, was the *Somme*, which I had earlier seen passing upstream through Amfreville lock.

Facing the Bassin aux Petroles is the little village of Croisset, now part of maritime Rouen. My eye was caught by a small square building. It was, I was told, the Flaubert museum. Of Rouen's novelists, Gide is not recalled locally with any pleasure. Maupassant has a small street called after him. But Flaubert has an avenue, a street and two museums. One is in his birthplace (his father was a surgeon at the local hospital), the other in the little pavilion at Croisset. Neither is really worth a visit. The pavilion is all that remains of the house beside the Seine where he lived with his mother, his sister and his niece. There, night after night, year after year, he would sit at the round table in the living-room, wrestling with *Madame Bovary*, writing and tearing up, trying to combine a clinical realism with his own innate romantic lyricism; and as the dawn seeped round the curtains, having completed perhaps one page after six or seven hours of work, he would haul himself off to bed, pausing on the way to be sick in the bathroom. I was sad that the room, the house have disappeared. The very walls, I felt, would still have been impregnated with the suffering and the effort of that long and lonely struggle.

Everything remains, however, of Corneille's house near the Vieux Marché. It is a prosperous bourgeois house, half-timbered, carefully restored in 1912 and undamaged during the war. Here the playwright was born, and lived most of his working life. Here he wrote his plays; the rooms are full of books and desks and engravings. The great classicist looks down on you from every wall. Is there any other writer who had his portrait painted as often as Corneille?

In the city of Flaubert and Gide it is as startling to meet Corneille as it is to encounter Poussin in the Impressionist country. In the world of the naturalistic novel it is salutary to remember the rigid world of classical literature; to be reminded of a time when it was unthinkable to write anything but five-act tragedies set in ancient Rome, written in Alexandrines, with male and female rhymes in alternate couplets and the climax of the play coming on the middle line of the middle act. Corneille was a Norman bourgeois, he lived amongt them, but it never occurred to him to portray their humours and follies, as it did to his friend Molière. It would have been no more possible for Corneille to have written about Monsieur Homais or the Heurtevent family than for Poussin to paint the barges on the Seine. But unlike Poussin, who emigrated to Rome, Corneille stayed beside the Seine. He practised as a lawyer in Rouen, meeting his Norman friends, participating in the local life. But his creative imagination was far away, buried, except for a famous excursion to medieval Spain, in the classical never-never land.

I left Corneille's house and walked across the Vieux Marché yet again and on down the rue du Gros Horloge. Joan of Arc, Corneille, Flaubert, American bombs – Rouen is a slice through the layer-cake of time. I had seen the crypt where William the Conqueror died; I had gazed in at the windows of International Business Machines and Burroughs and Roneo, all within a few yards of each other. And at the end of the street, at the end of every street it seemed, was the cathedral, dominating old Rouen and new Rouen alike.

Rouen cathedral is probably the most extreme example of Flamboyant Gothic anywhere. Every available square inch is en-crusted with carvings and pinnacles and statues; it is the architec-tural equivalent of Norman cooking, you keep adding more and more things to make it richer and better. It can be easily dismissed as fussy and over-ornate, but this is to miss the point. The Rouen

churches – the cathedral and the neighbouring churches of Saint-
Maclou and Saint-Ouen – are, deliberately, the apotheosis of in-
tricacy and detail. Those to whom architectual beauty is synony-
mous with functionalism, austerity, clean lines, graceful sweeps of
stone, proportion, harmony, symmetry should go elsewhere.

Perhaps there is an eastern influence here, a legacy of the Cru-
sades, for the Arabs too believed that elaborate pattern, complicated interweaving designs are beautiful and necessary to a place
of worship. Roulland le Roux, the master mason who built the
cathedral's central doorway and the top storey of the lantern
tower, also built the Bureau des Finances, a plain Renaissance
building opposite. Rich decoration was not applied automatically,
it would not have been appropriate on such a building. Detail was
for higher things.

The art of the Rouen masons was to take the heaviest and most
earthbound of materials, stone, and build it into towers of frothy
confectionery, tier upon tier of lace and lightness, so that they
seem to float in the still air. Can they really be made of stone, we
ask ourselves, Norman stone, the same stone as Westminster
Abbey?

The tower which dominates old Rouen, which seems to be at
the end of every street, is the Butter Tower of the cathedral. It got
this name, they say, because it was built out of funds paid by the
faithful for a special dispensation to be allowed to continue eating
butter and cream during Lent. Fasting is a deeply distressing
experience for Normans, and they must have paid handsomely for
the privilege, though apparently not quite enough to give the
tower a spire. Up and up goes the Butter Tower in an ecstasy of
detail until it reaches the summit crown.

Even more elaborate is the great lantern-tower which supports
the spire. But the finest of the three is the lantern tower of Saint-
Ouen, a marvel of levitation, with its crown suspended in the sky
above the square tower.

Considered as a building it must be admitted that the cathedral
itself is a mess. Indeed, it should really be considered as a huddle
of adjoining buildings. The south side was badly damaged in the
war and is now being carefully restored. But the huge west

façade was undamaged; nothing happened to lessen its power to amaze.

It is all here, portals, pinnacles, statues, gables, lattices, Trees of Jesse, interweaving foliage, Arab art, butter, cream, calvados, the lot. No other building can have such a variety of planes and surfaces, some catching the light, some in shadow, some washed clean by rain, some sheltered and grimy. Monet painted this wall twenty times, not as an act of piety but because nothing else gave him such a rich pattern of shape and shadow. He painted it at every hour of the day, in every kind of light, 'Effet du Matin', 'Soleil Matinal', 'Plein Soleil', 'Temps Gris', from blue dawn to rose dusk. Five of them hang together now in the Jeu de Paume and once again we can look through his eyes and realize that for him that complication of plane and curve and shadow was neither a religious experience nor a masterpiece of art but simply a backdrop to the ever-shifting pageant of light. If only he could have seen it by night, flood-lit, as we can today, the most dramatic moment of all, revealing a whole new pattern of highlight and shadow! He might have been inspired to paint a whole new series of pictures of that façade. For Monet was a Norman and he shared the simple faith of the cathedral architects, Guillaume Pontifs, Roulland le Roux and the rest – the belief that you can never have too much of a good thing.

12

One of the unsolved puzzles of history is the Normans. The terrible winged-hats, the Vikings, were masters of the seas from the ninth till the eleventh century, defied only by the navy of King Alfred. France, England, Greenland, Iceland, America, the Mediterranean – the Vikings were everywhere in their drakkars, landing on the coasts, penetrating up the rivers, burning, pillaging, plundering. Monks, peasants, lords trembled before the fury of the Northmen.

In France, however, in less than a century, these savage pirates had turned into a constructive, coherent civilization, well-administered, devout, prosperous. There was a mysterious leaven at work which turned them so quickly from Norsemen to Normans, from church-burners to abbey-builders. It was not intrinsic in their natures; no such change took place in the Vikings who went to Greenland or Iceland or even England. The Norman civilization flowered only in northern France, and went from there to England, Sicily, the Middle East. Those destructive sea-terrorists suffered their amazing land-change only in the Seine valley.

What brought about the transformation? Christianity, the remains of a Roman civilization, an established Germanic peasant society? But the Norsemen met all these in England too and nothing remarkable happened to them there. The Danelaw never became another Normandy. When William the Conqueror landed at Pevensey he did not find another Norman army waiting to receive him. The Norman tide moved from France to England, and not the other way round. What was it that happened to the Vikings in France, and only in France?

We can only offer some possible answers. The first is the personality of Rollo, who signed the Treaty of the River Epte and became the first Duke of Normandy. It was he who turned the Norsemen towards building and not destroying, to speaking the French language, to Christianity (though this was often more a matter of expediency than faith; some Viking chiefs boasted that they had been baptized more than twenty times, lapsing again at a moment of tactical opportunity).

A second reason, perhaps, is that the Vikings landed, by reason of wind or current, more thickly in England than in France, and they remained there as Danes, a hard lump that the Saxon social system was unable to digest. But in France they were relatively thin on the ground, a dominant minority, and the lords ruled, often precariously, their French vassals and rebellious fellow Vikings – still followers rather than subjects – by establishing a feudal system. And above all they were forced to intermarry, for they did not often bring their women with them in their exposed open drakkars. Rollo began it by marrying Gisèle of France, and the others followed his example, generation after generation, till by the year 1000 a young Norman count, brought up by his French mother, speaking French, attending mass, marrying a French wife, was not only culturally different from his Viking ancestors, he was racially different too. William the Conqueror, the illegitimate son of Duke Robert the Magnificent and Arlette, the humble washergirl of Falaise, had only a meagre trickle of Norse blood in his veins.

All this was due to chance and wind. If Rollo had landed in Yorkshire, if the Danes had been thin on the ground there and dense in France, if the Norman civilization had flowered on the Ouse and not on the Seine, the history of Europe, the languages of France and England, would now be very different. But there is one more factor which worked on the Danes in France which was not due to chance or wind.

Across northern France were scattered a number of monasteries, founded in the seventh and eighth centuries by such men as Saint Ouen and Saint Wandrille. These monasteries were not only centres of devotion, often housing sacred relics, but also centres of learning. The monks were scholars as well, in touch with other scholars elsewhere in France and Germany, speaking Latin and continuing the tradition of Roman literature and thought. Nothing comparable existed in England, though King Alfred himself was a cultured man and his court a centre of learning.

The Vikings, of course, dispersed the French monasteries, burning the abbeys, and forcing the monks to flee, carrying their manuscripts and their relics with them. But their value remained. The Norsemen were impressed by their learning and, though there was never such a thing as an intellectual Norman baron, they were prepared to encourage it in others. It was the Dukes of Normandy who instigated the Benedictine flowering of the eleventh century, who brought the abbot of Saint-Benigne at Dijon to Fécamp, who rebuilt, amongst others, the abbeys of Jumièges and Fontenelle, and re-established the monasteries.

The most spectacular results of this lie on the road from Rouen to the sea called La Route des Abbayes. The first on the Route Saint-Ouen in Rouen, is easily the largest and most splendid.

Saint Ouen himself was originally a courtier of King Dagobert (the one who, in the rhyme, put his trousers on back to front) and he became Bishop of Rouen in 641, playing a leading part in the city's ecclesiastical and civil affairs for the next forty-three years. The abbey church that we see today dates from the fourteenth and fifteenth centuries (except for the west front which was regrettably replaced in the nineteenth century in the cause of homogeneity). The outside is rich with pinnacles and flying-buttresses, the lantern tower a delirium of decoration, but inside all is simplicity and proportion and light. It is the longest of the Seine churches, longer than the cathedral or Notre Dame. The nave is the tallest in France after Beauvais cathedral. The columns soar away to the zenith, barely connected to the earth. It is one of the great Gothic masterpieces and a noble start to the Route des Abbayes.

13

The boat for La Bouille leaves from the Quai de la Bourse and it was here, after the execution on 30 May 1431, that the ashes and the pure unburnt heart of Joan of Arc were thrown into the Seine. This choice of a final resting place for the maid struck me as being entirely suitable. Whilst one could never have thought of her as a river-goddess, I felt that Sequana would have approved. Indeed, the two girls might have found a lot in common if they could ever have met.

But now, as we pulled away from the quay and moved downstream, there were other things in my mind besides Joan. Behind us rose up the churches, on either side were the cargo ships from Rotterdam, Hamburg, Dundee. The quays were straddled by giraffe-like cranes; ahead was Canteleu and the forest of Roumare. In my face was the sharp stench from the refineries at Petit-Couronne. It was Total Rouen.

There is a local saying, 'He who has not seen La Bouille has not seen anything.' And indeed La Bouille is charming. Set on the

next bend of the Seine, under a steep wooded hill, it has a picturesque old water-front, a pretty square, an old church with a tall
spire, several good restaurants. As scenery it is delightful.

As a place to stay it was disappointing. The food was excellent,
but I was rushed through it as if I had a train to catch, and that is
no way to treat a Norman dinner.

'What's the hurry?' I asked the waitress.

She looked at me stonily. She had not forgiven me for arriving
by boat instead of by car. 'I have my work to get on with,' she
said.

'But I am your work,' I said. 'There is nobody else staying here.'

After dinner I felt like stretching my legs by the river, watching
the water, smoking a last pipe, sipping a last drink. But instead I
was bundled off to bed at half-past nine, protesting like a school-
boy, the lights were put out and the doors locked.

'What do people do in La Bouille?' I asked the proprietor of a
water-front café the next morning. It was sunny and there was,
unexpectedly, a green cockatoo on the next chair, gazing at me
balefully. 'Do they sail, row, shoot?'

He shook his head. 'They have lunch and they drive on.'

'Do many people come out from Rouen?'

He shook his head. 'It is much too near. Anyway they all have
country cottages or seaside villas for the week-end.'

'But La Bouille is so pretty!'

He shook his head. 'It is not so pretty since the Germans
cemented the opposite bank.'

'Why did they do that?'

He shook his head sadly. 'They had la maladie du ciment.'

The Seine in these parts is a very different river from the Seine
I knew so well. Gone is the placid lake of the upper reaches; the
water rushes madly upstream or downstream with the tide; it has
changed its name once more. It is no longer la Seine, but la Basse
Seine. Barges are fewer, and the fishermen, those indestructible
river-folk, have gone with the washerwomen; no fish can live in
the water polluted by Rouen.

Instead there are the sea-going cargo ships, enormous vessels
proceeding slowly and improbably through the rural landscape,

completely out of place and out of proportion to the apple-trees and the cottages. I sat with the cockatoo and watched the ships sail by.

In a small winding side street I found a shop which sold glasses of cider from the barrel. Could I buy one, I asked.

Madame refused curtly. That was for the locals, not for étrangers. La Bouille is not a very welcoming place, but I persevered. If I bought a bottle of her cidre bouché, would she let me taste her cider from the barrel? In the end I won. She grudgingly gave me a glass; it was flat and full of apples, not nearly as strong or as sour as I had expected.

Then I walked up the hill to the castle of Robert le Diable. It was a lovely walk through beechwoods. The grass on the verges had just been cut and the world smelt of hay. Below me were orchards, a cheese factory, several fine châteaux standing in parkland, big ships. On the skyline was an unbroken green line of forest, and the dirty sky above Rouen.

Robert le Diable was apparently the same as Robert the Magnificent, but it is not known for sure whether he or an earlier Duke of Normandy built the castle. It has been well restored as a tourist attraction. In the courtyard is a full-scale model of a drakkar – and what uncomfortable ships they must have been for transatlantic voyages! The little rooms in the tower and in the cellars are filled with waxworks of the more famous Normans. The castle is spectacularly sited. From the top of the tower I had a magnificent view: on one side the Seine valley all the way from La Bouille to Rouen, on the other side an undulating seamless carpet of forest as far as the eye could see. I had not realized till then just how enormous the forests of Normandy are.

Downstairs, outside the castle gate, I found rosé de Provence, and an excellent home-made chicken liver pâté. Afterwards I was glad to be offered a lift back to La Bouille on the back of a workmen's lorry. It was a breakneck journey and we did it in about two minutes. The hotel waitress glared at me as I scrambled off the lorry, dusting myself. I was committing the unforgivable sin, I was lowering her *standing*.

14

Duclair, on the next bend of the river, is famous for its duckling. It also has a well-known restaurant run by the maître-rôtisseur, Bob Bucher. What, I asked Monsieur Bob, was so special about Duclair ducklings?

He pointed across the river at the flat woods and fields. That, he explained, was the first resting place the wild duck found when they flew in from the sea; everything else suitable was now an oil refinery. And from there they would fly across the river and see the domestic Duclair female ducks, sitting beside their pens hoping to be noticed, and would mate with them and breed a duck leaner and tastier than the pure domestic brand.

'Just like the Norsemen,' I commented. 'Arriving from across the seas, leaving their own women behind, mating with the local girls, producing a splendid new race. But how sad for the females left behind.'

I had of course to eat duckling in Duclair, but I couldn't face it à la Rouennais again. So I ordered caneton Topolinsky; Monsieur Bob had studied cooking under Topolinsky at Lapérouse in Paris. The duckling has a thick rich cheese sauce made from Gruyère and Parmesan. Indeed, I thought it a pretty cosmopolitan dish: a French rôtisseur, a Polish recipe, Swiss and Italian cheeses, international ducks. A great orange full moon was rising over the Seine, and the food was brought to me by another Norman blonde, a girl with huge eyes who whispered excitedly:

'M'sieu, votre caneton est préparé!'

Moons and girls and gastronomy apart, Duclair is less attractive than La Bouille, the waterfront less pleasing. But there is a quay shaded by lime-trees and there are the usual cliffs, the usual fine viewpoint behind the town. I could not help wishing that the villages were sometimes on the convex side of the bend so that you looked across at the hill and the cliffs, instead of having them always behind you. But of course this was impossible. The villages, being river-ports, would always be on the deep side of the river, under the cliffs, rather than on the flat shelving side.

Duclair was the point on the Seine where I first noticed how close we were getting to the sea. There were seagulls on the river, shrimps on the menu and in the air was the faint smell of the sea, except for those moments when a ship went by and stirred up the sulphurous depths with its screw.

Behind the waterfront is a little old church dating from the twelfth century. It has some fourteenth-century glass showing Saint Denis undergoing a complicated series of executions. I was interested to observe the etiquette for portraying a decapitated bishop. The right hand is raised in blessing, the left holds the head. The mitre remains on the severed head, but the halo is placed in the air above where the head used to be.

In the church were also a number of statues of the apostles, taken from Jumièges. These obviously were portraits, life-size, of the monks of Jumièges, carved in fourteenth-century stone. They had been placed on pedestals to give them modern height, but they were tiny men, thin, ascetic and intelligent; the opposite extreme from the pictures of fat jolly monks, painted on wooden cut-outs, who stand today outside the restaurants of the Route des Abbayes, holding menus.

15

The Route des Abbayes runs from Rouen through Duclair to Caudebec and beyond; and three of its most famous abbeys are in the neighbourhood of Duclair. The first, Saint-Martin-de-Boscherville, is the only one to have escaped destruction. It is a modest, plain Norman church dating from the eleventh century, and you can see its steeple from all the neighbouring viewpoints.

Jumièges is much older, one of the pre-Viking abbeys, founded in the seventh century. It was totally destroyed by the Norsemen and rebuilt by the Normans, William the Conqueror himself attending its consecration in 1067. It became a great centre of learning and good works, continuing for hundreds of years till the monks were driven out at the Revolution and the abbey was sold to a timber merchant of Rouen who used it as a warehouse. A combination of active destruction and neglect, which lasted till 1830, reduced it to a complete ruin once more. It is now preserved like that, the nave roofless, the towers steepleless, grass in the choir.

But it is a very beautiful ruin, much photographed, especially in the autumn. The pictorial eye can make lovely patterns of columns and arches and shadows and beeches and yews and spinning sycamore seeds. The setting, in a bend of the Seine, is perfect. The towers, more than a hundred and fifty feet high, rise up to the sky, the great columns of the nave still stand, thick and strong, a wall of the lantern tower bestrides space, framed by air. The stone is warm and golden and over everything is the patina of romantic melancholy induced by a carefully preserved ruin. All that is missing is swans.

St Wandrille, a few miles away, suffered much the same fate. Wandrille himself, Wandrigisilus to his friends, was another of the knights of good King Dagobert who became a saint. (The third, Saint Eloi, the one who pointed out the king's sartorial error, does not seem to have founded an abbey.) Wandrille and his wife were one of the earliest known examples of a couple taking their honeymoon apart, the bride retiring to a convent and he to a monastery, though King Dagobert, who was far from convinced that this was an ideal future for his doughty knight, put a lot of obstacles in his way. The abbey which Wandrille founded became another great centre of learning, and its history was almost exactly the same as Jumièges. The abbey was destroyed but the cloisters survived, to be turned into a country house, the residence of the English Marquis of Stacpoole who built a grandiose gateway, and later the writer Maurice Mæterlinck. Now the monks are back, black-robed figures striding through the ruins, talking earnestly to young engaged couples, advising them perhaps to take their honeymoon together.

As a ruin St Wandrille is much less spectacular than Jumièges. The columns of the nave barely rise out of the grass. But I can acquire a romantic melancholy as well in a cloister, even an un-damaged one. Others may pause to admire the decorated Renaissance lavabo where the monks once washed their hands before going to the refectory, or the fourteenth-century Madonna. But my ears were cocked for the distant sound of Gregorian chanting, my eyes followed the thin black-robed figures as they walked round the cloister, passing through the group of tourists as if we did not exist, on their way to the chapel or the workshops.

'They do not only pray, you know,' said my neighbour ap-provingly. 'They really *work*! They make excellent furniture polish. We can buy some on our way out.'

The imminent prospect of buying furniture polish, alas, proved fatal to my romantic melancholy. But the thought itself was sad enough; the long slide of the monastic ideal, of the abbey which Saint Wandrille founded at Fontenelle, from one of the foremost centres of learning in Christendom to a small firm manufacturing furniture polish.

Abbeys, abbeys all the way. But I was well nourished on my journey; the Route des Abbayes is not a pilgrimage to be under-taken fasting. Even the most modest restaurants placed before me course after course of gargantuan dishes; andouilles de Vire, stuffed mussels, crabs, pintadeau a l'estragon, poulet vallée d'Auge, canard à l'orange, coq aux tripes, Pont l'Evêque, Livarot, Neufchâtel, melons, peaches, grapes passed before my dazed eyes, my failing appetite, like an expressionist film. Never have I been more grate-ful for le trou Normand, that gap in the middle of the meal when you gulp down a glass of calvados, mop your forehead, take a deep breath and summon back your courage for the second half. As I staggered away, thinking regretfully of my thickening figure, I would remember that I was after all only eating the ordinary menu touristique. Heaven help me if I should raise my sights and try the menu gastronomique!

In the evenings I would sit in the local cafés, all bleak striplight-ing and friendly faces, waiting for the bus to take me back to Duclair or Caudebec. My mind might be full of broken columns, my stomach full of cream, but my eyes would be riveted by the posters on the walls: 'Jazz Club Modern. En Attraction: Les

Mystères.' Or I would gaze lasciviously at a photograph of the rich curves and dark beauty of a girl with the aristocratic name of Caroline de Beaumont, who was apparently an all-in wrestler. Or I would watch the people.

They were short, dark, long-nosed, thick with the opposite of malnutrition, vivacious, smiling, talkative. They were typical Franks. Kind hearts were here in plenty but where was the Norman blood? Everyone in Normandy seems to be called Leroux, but where were the red-heads, the fair-heads? I had so far met exactly two blondes, Catherine in Amfreville and Martine in Duclair, both decoratively behind bars. Were they the only two, the last survivors of Norse stock? Were there any remaining traces of the Viking invasions, I wondered, except abbey ruins and a lingering instinct for gluttony?

16

Caudebec-en-Caux is much larger than the usual Seine village and indeed is the capital of the Pays de Caux. It used to be inhabited, I was told, by hundreds of Huguenot beaver-hat makers who fled at the Revocation of the Edict of Nantes. After that it was forgotten and remained untouched, a little old town of timbered houses and winding streets, so old that one even had a stream running down the middle. Picturesque old inflammable houses – the temptation was too great and the Germans set fire to it in 1940 like Old Rouen. The Seine valley has suffered much from the German fondness for seeing everything go up in flames at the end of the opera.

The stone church and three adjoining houses alone survived. The church is large and old and almost counts as an abbey. Henri IV called it the most beautiful chapel in the kingdom. Its belfry with an elaborate triple crown dominates the town and the inside is full of good things: stalls and statues from Jumièges and Saint-Wandrille, a fine rose window, some old glass with glowing reds and greens which somehow survived the holocaust, a vault with a large hanging keystone weighing seven tons, a triumph of look-no-hands architecture.

The town has been rebuilt in uniform traditional style, each block looking exactly like the next. But the steep tiled roofs are a pleasing feature and will weather attractively, and the gardens were full of hydrangeas. I have no doubt that the inhabitants much prefer it as it is now.

The great tourist attraction of Caudebec used to be, apart from the old streets, the mascaret, the bore or tidal wave which came up the river twice a day, three days at a time, four times a year in February, March, August and September. It was the highest of high tides arriving in one wave, full of mud, moving at fifteen kilometres an hour. It caused a thrilling number of wrecks, drownings and broken limbs and tourists would come from far and wide to see it, lining the banks with their cameras, daring the wave to get them, like children at the seaside. The police would clear the water-front, but there was always some camera-mad daredevil to duck under their arms and rush back to the quay, to disappear for ever. The most recent case was a newly married girl in 1961 who was never recovered from the mud.

In August 1940 large numbers of German soldiers drove up to see the sight, and lined the bank, Leicas at the ready, grinning in anticipation. Caudebec had only recently been burnt and the population gazed at them in stony silence.

'Did nobody warn them?' I asked.

My informant, the pilot of the launch taking me to Villequier, said, 'We didn't say a word'. He added, 'But none of them were drowned. There were some broken legs and arms, but they were all saved. All their cameras were lost, though.'

'I suppose you all laughed,' I said.

'We didn't say a word.'

But the mascaret doesn't come any more, not since the estuary channel was altered. Caudebec's second tourist attraction has gone like the first. A superstition that it will return every seven years is being carefully nourished locally, but it has yet to be tested.

17

It was pouring with rain when I landed at the pilots' jetty at Villequier and I took hasty shelter in the pilots' rest house. The concierge told me I could sit in the lounge. 'But you will have to get used to rain in Villequier,' she added cryptically. I could not see why the weather in Villequier should be any wetter than in Caudebec a mile or two away, but I was at the moment not well placed for arguing the point.

I asked where the pilots were, were they asleep upstairs?

'If you like,' the concierge answered mysteriously, 'but it is not obligatory.'

It dawned on me that she must think I was a fresh pilot arrived for a spell of duty, wanting to sleep before I guided a ship on its journey. I wondered what she made of my accent; Flemish perhaps.

Villequier is the point where the estuary pilots hand over to river pilots, or vice versa, and watching the pilots change is the great activity of the village. Nothing happens for hours on end while the tide rises and then suddenly the river is full of sea-going ships, slowed down but not stopping. It is a hectic time, the impatient ships hoot like angry elephants, the launches dash to and fro, their searchlights shaking, tiny pilots scramble up and down rope ladders.

The other activity of visitors to Villequier is visiting the Victor Hugo museum in the Maison Vacquerie beside the river. After the fiasco of his tragedy *Hernani*, Hugo was consoled by the admiration of the two young Vacquerie brothers in Paris. He was badly in need of admiration and anyway he liked young disciples. The brothers invited him to come and stay at their family house in Villequier. He came, and the place and the family appealed to him. His romantic spirit enjoyed the river, the hills and the woods, and he took to spending his holidays there. He wrote on one occasion to Vacquerie that he longed to be once more 'beside your woods, beside your waters, under your great trees'.

In due course young Charles Vacquerie married Hugo's daughter Léopoldine. Seven months later, on 4 September 1843, they were out sailing in a boat made by Charles, and they capsized. It was not due to the mascaret, but to ordinary Villequier summer weather. Nowadays girls sailing on the Seine wear life-jackets and shorts, but Léopoldine was less lightly dressed and she could not swim. Her husband, who could swim, tried to save her, but in vain. They were both drowned.

The loss of a loved one often proved disastrous to members of the Hugo family. At Victor's wedding, his brother Eugène, who turned out to be secretly in love with the bride, went violently mad and spent the rest of his life in the Charenton asylum. In 1872 Hugo's other daughter, Adèle, went mad after the death of her English husband and spent the rest of her life in the Suresnes asylum. And now after Léopoldine's death Hugo and his wife went almost out of their minds for three days. Madame Hugo shrieked all night, her hands twisting continually the dead girl's hair. 'Victor Hugo looks ten years older,' wrote Balzac.

Hugo was overwhelmed by grief and remorse, for he regarded the accident as a punishment for his infidelities to his wife. He was so numbed by his sense of loss and bereavement that he published nothing more for ten years. (Though it must be admitted there were other reasons too. Hugo was turning away from romantic drama towards socialism, political pamphleteering and *Les Misérables*.) In 1856 he published his *Contemplations*, probably the finest fruit of his lyric genius. 'Yesterday, today, an abyss separates them, the tomb,' he wrote, and the tomb was Léopoldine's at Villequier. The book contained the famous poem, 'À Villequier', in which he poured out his grief, his reproaches to God, his resignation to fate. And while one can be greatly moved by his heart-broken eloquence, his passion, his Job-like submission, his falling cadences, one cannot help feeling that he was a good deal sorrier for himself than for poor Léopoldine. In the Maison Vacquerie is the manuscript of another poem Hugo wrote on her loss, full of sadness and desolation, and many people, including for a while the museum itself, have been deceived into thinking that he wrote it too after her death. In fact he wrote it on the occasion of her marriage.

I could not share Hugo's enthusiasm for Villequier as a resort. Despite the hills and the beechwoods, despite some truly great trees, including a splendid magnolia, I thought it a poor place, not to be compared with Les Andelys or La Bouille. Perhaps it looked better in his day, perhaps there was a line of pretty houses along the water-front, and not the straggle of Victorian villas there is today.

Drains, garbage, refuse, trash, everything goes into the river at Villequier; there is apparently no organized form of rubbish disposal. All evening I watched housewives and children carrying down buckets of garbage and emptying them on to the mud flats and the river bank. The rising tide then washed it away upstream to deposit it on the shore at Caudebec, which seemed bad luck on that clean and proud little town. But plenty remains at Villequier, and at low tide the mud-flats are nauseating to the eye and nose, littered for some reason with the skulls and bones of long-dead cattle. It was no way, I felt, to treat a great river.

I felt, too, alienated for once from the Seine itself. It was now a great waterway, a sewer, something governed by winds and tides, something not to be trifled with. Drownings, tidal waves, wrecks, navigation beacons, ferries; but I could not help looking back rather nostalgically to the calm motionless Seine at Marcilly, troubled by little except fishermen, and even further back to the brook bubbling through the wild flowers of the Côte d'Or.

Full of unromantic melancholy I ate my dinner quickly. I was in no mood for gargantua, for le trou Normand. As I left the dining-room the proprietor handed me my key and wished me good night. It was not yet nine o'clock and I protested. I wished to stretch my legs and let my dinner go down. The patron looked at me suspiciously. Would I be gone long?

Perhaps half an hour, I said, as he unlocked the deserted bar and let me out like a cat. What was the matter, I asked. Was he scared of clients?

At this hour, certainly, he said. He had to be up early, he started serving breakfast at six o'clock.

'Why on earth?' I asked, but he shrugged and walked away.

One of my pleasures is to stroll to the local square after dinner, sit in a café, drink a last drink and watch the people, the lights, the wandering crowds. But this is a dream of the south, of Paris, even of Rouen. In Villequier there were no squares, no cafés, no people, no wandering crowds. Except for the street-lights, the whole place was already in darkness, including my hotel. I went and stood by the Seine, listening to the drumming of the rain on my umbrella. Occasionally a woman or a child who should have been in bed hours ago would creep by and empty another bucket of garbage into the river.

18

I was barely a mile from Villequier when the rain stopped and the sun came out, so perhaps wet weather is a local speciality. I recalled Gibbings complaining about the rain there. But to be away, back in the sunshine, back among the fields and orchards was an exhilarating experience. We were travelling along the top of an escarpment; to our left was a steep drop to a flat valley inter-sected at geometric intervals by straight lines of poplars like hedges. Beyond was the river and its shipping, and further off the green line of the Forêt de Brotonne. To our right was cosy Norman countryside with hedges, thatched cottages, apple trees and sheep grazing beneath them. It was peaceful, utterly rural, far from the industrial world – and then quite suddenly we saw Port Jerome.

The refineries of Port Jerome would be one of the remarkable sights of the Seine from any viewpoint, a dream of the twentieth century, a silver Antonioni landscape of towers and spheres and flames. But to see it in a Christmas-card setting, across thatch, framed by fruit-trees, was bizarre, two opposing cultures, aesthetics, ideals muddled together, forward-to-the-future over-printed on back-to-nature propaganda.

We came down off the escarpment and drove slowly round

Port Jerome. At close sight its beauty was breath-taking; huge aluminium spheres balanced on circles of spikes like coronets, hemispheres reflecting the sun, sculptured towers with delicate carving, gleaming chimneys like huge candles with bright orange flames on top. It was a fantastic achievement of contemporary art, a modern folly built by some avant-garde millionaire, a gigantic park of pavilions and sculpture. To think that it was also strictly functional, industrial, money-making was unbelievable.

Across the river by ferry from Port Jerome is the picturesque fishing port of Quillebeuf, a water-front of little old houses. Here the Vikings landed in their drakkars; here, it is said, the French crown jewels were sunk in 1790. But few boats now put to sea from Quillebeuf. Its inhabitants cross the ferry each day to work at Port Jerome.

Most of the labour for the refineries lives in the surrounding villages and in the market-town of Lillebonne. Lillebonne was originally Juliobona, called after the great Julius himself, the capital of the district and an important port with twenty-five thousand inhabitants. But the river changed its course, the port silted up and the importance and population of Lillebonne declined sharply. Now, with the rise of Port Jerome, it is beginning to grow again and new blocks of flats are sprouting over the old town.

However, it is not of Caesar that you think in Lillebonne, but of that other later conqueror, William. It was here that he assembled his barons to persuade them to follow him in his forthcoming invasion of England. It must have been a hair-raising meeting. Few of the barons wanted to risk everything on the English adventure, many of them had no wish to see William the Bastard become King of England or even remain as Duke of Normandy. A murder could so easily have been arranged.

The castle is on the hill which dominates Lillebonne. Here was the Roman fort, William's castle. Here Henry II of England stayed in his capacity as Duke of Normandy, and here Philippe Auguste raised his standard after the French reconquest of Normandy. Nothing now remains of William's castle except a fragment of the outer walls; the last ruins were demolished in 1830, but Philippe

Auguste's tower still stands, together with a fragment of an octagonal tower and a hideous Victorian house. Between them peacocks spread their tails, giving a note of the exotic to a historic place.

I climbed the 109 steps of the tower, and from the top I could see the marks of the three stages in the history of Lillebonne: the Roman theatre, the Norman castle, the modern blocks of flats. But I could no longer see the Seine.

I clicked back almost a thousand years from William and went to see the Roman theatre. It dates from the second century and it could, they say, hold three thousand people. I tried to say something appropriate, to declaim some Latin lines, but all I could recall was a poem starting 'A, ab, absque, coram, de'. So I recited that. It is not a very interesting poem, but then it is not a very interesting theatre.

Despite Rotomagus, despite Juliobona, there are few notable traces of the Roman occupation in the Seine valley: a piece of wall here, a few coins there. It is not like the Rhône. There is no great arena, no Pont du Gard, no Maison Carrée. But the traveller sees and hears the word Roman all the way. This is, of course, a well-known catch. *Roman* is the French for Romanesque, what in England would be called Saxon or Norman. The French for Roman is *Romain*. But it takes an alert ear attuned to the Norman voice to detect which your informant is saying, or even if he is saying Rouen. All three words are pronounced as mono-syllables.

In the square beside the theatre I sat in the sun outside a café, drinking beer, waiting for my bus. It was a moment for beer, for I was suddenly feeling, not Roman but Scandinavian. I was in Viking-land at last. The square was full of tall fair men, blonde girls. Looking at the people at the nearby tables, the queue waiting for the bus, I could have thought myself in Copenhagen.

19

Just beyond Quillebeuf the Seine makes its last bend and then straightens out into the estuary. The cliffs recede, the landscape flattens into marshland. But one last cliff remains, the nez of Tancarville. Surmounted by an eighteenth-century castle and the ruins of an eleventh-century one, this promontory is a gatepost of the Seine. And from its summit there springs out like a high dive the great Tancarville suspension bridge.

This vast and beautiful bridge dominates the whole landscape; I had seen it in the distance from Quillebeuf. It is one of the largest suspension bridges in Europe, 4,593 feet long; the central span is almost two thousand feet long, a thread of scarlet hanging in air 156 feet above high-tide level.

It was opened in 1959, the only bridge below Rouen. Before that date all traffic from one side of Normandy to the other, from Le Havre and Dieppe to Caen and Cherbourg, had either to make the long detour by Rouen or use one of the ferries, which is often a slow and difficult business. Anyway they do not work at night. Now at last the two halves of Normandy were joined together, the ancient frontier between the Belgae and the Armoricae finally breached.

There is, of course, a fine view from the middle of the bridge; indeed, one of the problems is the number of pedestrians and motorists who stop there to gaze at the panorama, and to photograph the sharp patterns and perspective of the bridge itself, like me. Upstream was the familiar Seine valley, the hills and fields, the flames of Port Jerome. Downstream was the estuary, the marshes. In the distance were the smoke of the chimneys of Le Havre, the cliffs of Honfleur, and the gleaming line of the Channel. Below me, on the wide brown ribbon was shipping. But I could not help thinking of the first bridge on the Seine, that little brick arch carrying a path over a stream four inches wide.

A man interrupted my reverie. 'Excuse me, but is that the Seine?'

I judged him from his accent to be Canadian. 'Yes,' I said.

He stared at it for a moment and then shook his head. 'No, it isn't. The Seine is smaller than that. I've seen it before, you see.' I let it go.

Apart from its achievements as a piece of engineering, I felt bound to admit that the last bridge is far more beautiful than the first. Indeed, the view of the bridge itself is to be preferred to the view from the bridge. I watched it through the changing light of the day's cycle with wonder; its shape seemed to change all the time. In daylight the dominating feature is the two suspension ropes, swooping down from the top of one pylon to the roadway and up to the top of the other pylon. At night the ropes disappear and the bridge becomes two floodlit pylons, like gigantic white letter 'A's four hundred feet high. After the floodlighting is turned off, all that can be seen is the line of street-lamps on the bridge, a gentle curve like a bow. And in the dawn, with the valley full of river mist, nothing except two red beaconlights shining far above.

Gargantua struck again at Tancarville, struck as never before. The Hotel de la Marine is superbly placed beside the bridge, but Monsieur Morisse, the proprietor, does not rest on the view; he knows perfectly well that you haven't come to admire the bridge but to eat: filets de sole Tancarville, éclair au jambon, boudin de Saint-Romain flambé au calvados, poulet flambé au calvados, canard à l'orange; any or all of them. You are expected to eat five huge courses, and the choice is vast, the price low.

Drinking arrangements are equally copious. Unless you opt out the price includes three magnums – not bottles, magnums – of Macon which are placed on each table, one each of white, rosé and red, and opened.

Madame Églantine, the sister of Monsieur Morisse, was wandering round the tables, talking to the guests, kissing the more flirtatious ones. 'Am I expected to drink all that?' I asked her.

'I hope you will,' she said.

I changed my line. 'And if it is not enough?'

'Then I will bring you some more.'

It was, I found, excellent wine, far better than many more pretentious vintages. And looking round the restaurant, at table after table covered with these enormous bottles, I thought Vix had nothing on this. At one meal I told the waitress that she need not open the rosé as I would be confining myself to the white and red for this meal. But she firmly opened the rosé as well, 'so that you can change your mind without difficulty.'

However, nobody was drunk. There were stories that someone had once finished all three magnums, but the details were very vague. Normans are moderate drinkers; indeed, I noticed one couple washing down their great meal with nothing more than a half bottle of Beaujolais between them. You do not go to Tancarville to drink, you go to eat.

It seemed as if the whole of Le Havre came out to lunch there on Sunday. Tables overflowed into every room. The couple at the table on my left had the same table every Sunday. The man told me that he used to come out at week-ends to shoot; the estuary marshes were free and there was plenty of duck and wild geese. But now all these had gone, perhaps due to the fumes from the refineries, or possibly to overshooting. So now he just came to eat.

'Les Normands sont très gourmands,' he said happily. It was a phrase I had heard before.

On the other side were a father, mother and son, three of the largest people I had ever seen and growing visibly before my eyes. They too had the same table every Sunday. But neither of my two neighbours had ever spoken to each other. You do not come to Tancarville to talk.

Large family parties would come and spend the day there, the grandmother wearing local headdress, the children doggedly chewing their way through the long meal. Afterwards the grown-ups sat in the garden, watching the river and a lawn with a sunken boat full of flowers, a sight which would have pleased Robert Frost. The children would hang upside down from swings and horizontal bars, for hours on end without being sick. As the evening drew in they would regroup round the same table in the restaurant, ready to do it all over again. Stamina, that is the great Norman quality.

After dinner Monsieur Morisse, who did the cooking himself,

joined me in the bar. He accepted a soft drink and remained standing. Once he sat down, he explained, he would not have the strength to get up again. Indeed, after the long and crowded day it was no wonder if he looked tired and pale. In sharp contrast there was a photograph of him over the bar with black face, curly hair, ear-rings and gleaming eyes; a sultry if, even then, slightly melancholy Moor.

I had heard that he had been an internationally distinguished tenor before coming to Tancarville. Was it true, I asked, that Otello was a cruel part for the voice?

'Oui, c'est très dur,' he agreed. It was a fine part, but not one that he preferred. We spoke of other parts that he had sung: Cavaradossi, Radames, Don José. Lohengrin. I asked him which part was his favourite, the one he would choose to sing above all others.

'Werther,' he said. 'Above all, Werther. It is the role with which I find myself most in sympathy.'

I found it strange that this man who had achieved such notable success in two such different careers should wish to identify himself with the unhappy Werther.

I lingered at Tancarville. I was lured by the modern bridge, the glittering lights and smoky flames of Port Jerome, and, in total contrast, the desolate marshes, devoid even of swans and geese and plover. I was also, I frankly admit it, growing lethargic. To catch the bus to Le Havre involved walking up on to the nez, carrying my suitcase, standing at the bus-stop at the end of the bridge. It was easier to postpone departure by one more day; there was no hurry, I should not starve. My condition, I realized, was like that of an Antarctic explorer who finds himself sinking happily into a last euphoric sleep in the snow, never to move again.

Alert to the danger for a moment of truth, I found myself on the river bank, looking at a barge which had grounded on the mud-flat, while awaiting the opening of the lock into the Tancarville canal. A girl was playing with a baby beside the wheel-house. I shouted down, 'Are you going to Le Havre?'

An older woman peered out of the wheel-house. 'Tomorrow morning.'

'Can I come too?'

'Bien sûr. We shall be in the canal beyond the lock at nine o'clock.'

Madame Églantine took the news of my departure with some astonishment. She was used to people who came by car. She did not know what to make of one who came by bus and left by barge.

'Eh bien, I will drive you to the lock in my car,' she said. 'That will look better for the others.'

20

The barge was called, unromantically, *S.G.4* and unlike *Sacolève* did not belong to the bargee. It was owned by the big chemical company of Saint-Gobain and it carried sulphuric acid between Le Havre and Rouen. My host, Monsieur Roger Sarazin, being a tenant and not an owner, there was a slightly different atmosphere on board. Unlike the Lenoirs he was not free to choose his contracts and journeys; if necessary he had to do night work without days off. 'We never get time for fishing,' he commented. On the other hand, he got a month's paid holiday every year, while his barge was laid up in Rouen, something which the Lenoirs would never know.

S.G.4 was as immaculate as *Sacolève*, and it even had television. It was an old barge and quarters were cramped. Previously the Sarazins had been on a modern barge with more room, and they had made interesting journeys along the canals of Belgium, Holland, Germany and southern France. Now they only carried one cargo over one monotonous route, but they were quite content. The money was much better.

There seemed to be an awful lot of people on board. The Sarazins had eight children, all born on board, named in pairs, Jacques and Jacqueline, Bernard and Bernadette, and so on.

'When you have chosen a name,' said Madame Sarazin, a large freckled woman, 'you want to get full use out of it.'

The youngest, Bernadette, was three, and Madame Sarazin was stopping there. 'Now we shall have to wait for the grandchildren,' she said. She hadn't had long to wait. Jacqueline, who looked about seventeen, had married a garçon de terre, a locksmith in some northern town, but she had returned to the barge for a holiday with her baby, Bruno.

In order to keep out of the way, I sat on a chair at the forward end of the barge. Gradually the whole family, except Monsieur Sarazin, who was at the wheel, came forward to talk to me. I was brought the baby to play with. Playing with babies is the great hobby of bargees and Bruno was the happiest of babies, burbling and chuckling with joy, adored by all his uncles and aunts, except perhaps by his Aunt Bernadette, who had just had her ears pierced and was rather sorry for herself. Unlike Madame Lenoir, Madame Sarazin did not believe in tying on children. She thought it was bad for them, and only made them want to escape and fall overboard, as had happened to a young nephew of hers. It was better to explain the dangers to them and leave them to be sensible. I dare say she was right psychologically, but there were moments when I trembled for the future of Bernadette.

Monsieur Sarazin was a true bargee. His mother had run away with a bargee to Belgium when she was only thirteen. She had returned with a baby the following year and been forgiven. She went on to have twenty-one more children, all born on barges; my host, Roger, was the seventeenth. Rather surprisingly he had married a fille de terre and Madame Sarazin admitted that she still hadn't quite got used to the life. Their eldest son, Bernard, had left home and worked on a pousseur. At that moment his pousseur passed us, going towards Rouen.

'Voilà Bernard! C'est Bernard!' We shouted and waved, he shouted and waved back, Bruno was held up for him to see, Bernadette danced with excitement, I took a photograph of him. I wonder who he thought I was.

The Tancarville canal cuts straight through the marshes to Le Havre, so that barges need not go out into the wide and often rough estuary. To either side were the flat wastes which should have been full of wild duck and geese and herons, but were so no longer. 'Sometimes in the winter,' said one of the boys, 'but not very many.'

We passed a camping site with a small bathing beach. Madame wrinkled up her nose in disgust. 'Fancy swimming in *that*!' she exclaimed, pointing to the filthy canal. Sometimes, it seemed, the water was so covered in oil that police launches had to patrol up and down making everyone put out all fires for fear of setting the whole canal on fire. They might have to go three days without a hot meal.

I thought of a question I had long wanted to ask. 'How do bargees manage on petrol barges where all smoking is permanently forbidden?'

They laughed. 'They smoke down below, out of sight! But never while loading or unloading.'

Behind me the view was still dominated by the Tancarville bridge. Ahead were factories, fields of cars, the plant where the natural gas from the Sahara arrived by ship, frozen to a temperature of minus 258 degrees Fahrenheit and diminished to one six-hundredth of its normal bulk. Then we were passing an oil refinery, its silver spheres and coronets and towers shining like spires in the August sunshine, and reflected in the oily waters of the canal. It was, I thought, the right way to arrive in Le Havre.

We passed Harfleur, once a harbour, a castle, the scene of Henry v's famous assault, and now a suburb of Le Havre. But nothing remains of the castle now; indeed, nothing remains of Harfleur, except an unexpected church spire in a landscape of pylons and warehouses and canals. Ahead were drawbridges, not for defence of the castle, but to carry roads across the canal. We hooted, and the bridges were raised, hanging in the air above us, dripping down our necks.

We came to a halt beside a wharf on which was a mountain of brilliant yellow sulphur several hundred feet high. Beside this improbable feature I said goodbye to my new friends, all ten of them.

21

Le Havre dates from the early sixteenth century. François I ordered a replacement to be found for Harfleur which was silting up, and Grand Admiral Bonnivet had noticed that the high tide lasted two hours longer at Le Havre than elsewhere on the coast. Otherwise it was a desolate marsh, and experts had to be brought from Venice to advise on methods of building on marshland. The king gave his approval and named the new port Le Havre de Grace. In 1518 his flagship entered the king's dock.

Thereafter it has been a story of great prosperity and terrible disasters, the last and worst being in September 1944 when the Germans decided not to surrender but to fight to the last. This condemned the harbour and the town centre to total destruction. Le Havre was known as the worst damaged port in Europe.

If the problems of clearing were immense, so were the opportunities. Le Havre could start once again, as in the days of François I. A modern port, a modern city could rise on the site. The French supplied money and the Allies materials; the architect Auguste Perret was put in charge of the rebuilding.

The result is much trumpeted: 'a masterpiece of town-planning', 'a triumph of city building in the mid-twentieth century', 'an example for all Europe'. The guide-books, the tourist leaflets, the posters are loud in the praise of the modern town and of Auguste Perret. And indeed there is much to admire in his cunning plan; the wide streets for modern traffic, the use of perspectives, the way, for instance, in the Boulevard François I, the seaward blocks are solid and square as windbreaks, while the leeward buildings are zigzagged to face the sun.

But modern! Anyone looking for another Brasilia, another Radiant City, will be disappointed. To see Le Havre today is to realize just what Le Corbusier was up against. The architecture is a triumph for traditional provincialism; even the Town Hall, the focal point, has columns, tentative columns like premature embryos. The blocks, whether for flats, hotels, shops or banks, are identical; four storeys high, brown-grey, lumpish, severe. It is a dispiriting sight.

A heavy atmosphere of austerity hangs over the town. The streets may be wide, but Le Havre is still the city of *La Porte Étroite*. The sad ghost of Alissa walks the boulevards, her mouth pursed in disapproval. And though the puritanism is now socialist rather than religious in its origin, the effect is the same. There is no theatre; it was destroyed and never rebuilt. The casino has been recently pulled down. The fair on the sea-front, the one splash of colour, is to be closed and replaced by a swimming-pool. There is, it is true, the Maison de la Culture which puts on exhibitions of Danish or African art, but few people go. There are few trees, cafés, gardens, playgrounds. Posters, neon signs, awnings, striped umbrellas are missing. So are the gay crowds, the people, the cars. The Avenue Foch, you are frequently told, is as wide as the Champs Elysées. But it will be a sad day for Paris if the Champs Elysées ever looks as dead as this.

The gardens of Saint-Roch, just off the Avenue Foch, close at seven every evening, so that businessmen cannot sit there after the offices close on a summer evening and enjoy the air. There are few gardens in Le Havre, but instead there are large numbers of small square or triangular tarmac piazzas whose purpose remains obscure. Walled in with low walls, they cannot be intended for parking. They have no seats, amenities or chairs and there is nothing you can do except walk across them quickly. They would make good company parade grounds. And indeed Le Havre reminds you of a barracks, with vague overtones of banks and railway stations.

Round the Place de l'Hotel de Ville, one of the biggest squares in Europe, are six buildings of ten storeys, but otherwise the same as the rest. 'C'est trop New-Yorkais,' said my taxi driver.

'If only it were!' I exclaimed. It was, I think, Miss Hermione Gingold who said that anything under sixty storeys was a sawn-off mess. The description filled exactly these blocks with their untidy skylines.

My complaint against Le Havre is that it is not modern enough.

The inhabitants dislike it for the opposite reason. Nobody lives in the new part if they can find anywhere else to live. Indeed, Le Havre is like a wheel, flinging everyone to the suburbs by centrifugal force. The lucky get flats in Caucriauville where a number of attractive new blocks are going up. The rich go to Sainte-Adresse, where on the hill overlooking the estuary and the Normandy coastline you can find an intriguing mixture of seaside architecture: Bournemouth gables, Spanish patios, Rhine castles, Norman cottages and Swiss chalets. These who have to live in the centre, until they find somewhere else to live, do their shopping in the outskirts, in the busy and squashed rond-point area. In the new streets the shops are empty or up for sale; the bars are closing; the wide streets intended for milling crowds and heavy traffic are deserted. The masterpiece of town-planning has become a ghost town.

I had an introduction to one of the leading businessmen of the town. He came originally from the south and was miserable in the grim north. The evening before, sick of watching television, he had gone for a walk along the Avenue Foch, with his wife. They had walked the length and back without passing a soul. But through the windows of every house they heard the television programme they were trying to avoid.

'After nine o'clock there is hardly a light in the town,' he said. 'Just the street-lights, and a few cafés on the Quai de Southampton waiting for the ferry to go out. The tourists arriving from England take one look round and drive out fast. How is that for tourism?'

I asked him why there were so many shops closed in a booming town.

'Booming town!' he laughed. Certainly the port was booming. It was the second port of France, and at the present rate of expansion and the present decline of Marseilles, it would be the first port in a few years. The crisis caused by the collapse of the cotton and coffee trades had been overcome; petrol, cars, electronic goods, machine tools, food had taken their place. The volume of imports and exports rose year by year. But not much of this rubbed off on to the city. The port was autonomous, it was mildly at war with the town. The ships did not stay long in port, it did not take many men to pump the petrol through to Paris.

But were there not big plans, I asked, to expand the city of Le Havre, to bring in new industries, to turn it into a major industrial conurbation?

Certainly there were, he said. Le Havre was ideally situated, with its harbour, its river and canal connections, its airport. Eventually, he felt sure, there would be factories all the way from Le Havre to Rouen. But in the meantime capitalists felt cautious about expanding in a zone controlled by a communist municipal council.

And in the meantime, I asked, what about Le Havre?

'They have the *France*,' he laughed. 'They have the yachting. And I shall retire to the Midi.'

I left his office and walked back down the rue de Paris to my hotel. The rue de Paris is the shopping centre of the new town, the same blocks but arcaded. The rue de Rivoli, it is said, of Le Havre. I walked the length of the street and I looked into every shop as I passed. I did not see a single customer.

If, I reflected, Hitler's orders had been obeyed and Paris burnt to the ground; if, as was quite possible, Auguste Perret had been commissioned to rebuild the capital, the real rue de Rivoli, the real Champs Elysées would now look like this. It was a sobering thought.

However, one building of new Le Havre requires mention, and that is the church of Saint-Joseph on the Boulevard François i. It is built in the same stone-and-concrete as the rest of the town and, indeed, it looks like a bank from the outside, except that its belfry is 350 feet high, startling in a squat town like Le Havre. The interior is very striking. The tower rises and rises to an etherial height, lit by stained-glass windows which are planned to maximize the light from the moving sun. The altar is in the centre of the church under the tower, on a platform under a modern canopy. Round it on all four sides are rows of tip-up cinema seats. The whole setting would be very suitable for a congress or a boxing-match. But the heating of the church is a great problem, as all the heated air rises immediately into the tower. So the small congregation huddles in the simple winter chapel, glassed off from the rest of the church like a television commentator's box.

I do not wish to sound too hostile. Saint-Joseph can hardly be called a success, but it is well worth a visit for the inside sight of the lantern tower. It is an interesting experiment, remarkable for such an unadventurous architect as Perret, and, it must be admitted, a not unworthy end to the Route des Abbayes.

22

Discouraged by Le Havre I crossed the river to Honfleur. It would be hard to find a greater contrast than the two ports at the mouth of the Seine; Honfleur, the historic transatlantic port which silted up, whose career came to an end about the time when Le Havre was starting. Le Havre full of big liners and tankers, Honfleur only now used by yachtsmen and fishermen who catch the celebrated Honfleur shrimps, the effort of peeling which totally overshadows the tiny taste at the end. Le Havre, ravaged and rebuilt; Honfleur spared by all wars, still a fifteenth-century town. Busy Le Havre with its streets deserted; sleepy Honfleur choked with cars and sightseers.

Honfleur is a delight to the eye. The streets are narrow and winding, the houses tall and timbered. Round the Vieux Bassin they are usually faced with slate, which might have looked dreary but in fact is most picturesque. I wandered along the quay looking at the houses opposite, all of different heights, the reflections in the water, the yachts which had all sailed across from England. At the end, on the Governor's House, La Lieutenance, is a plaque commemorating the voyages of Samuel de Champlain, the founder of Quebec and the first Governor-General of Canada.

Honfleur and Dieppe were the ports which supplied the great Norman voyages of exploration and colonization in the sixteenth and seventeenth centuries: Champlain in Canada, La Salle in Louisiana, Jean Ango and Verrazano at Manhattan Island. Verrazano reported that the site was entirely suitable for a large

new port, but François I was not much interested. He judged the
success of expeditions solely by whether they brought back gold
or diamonds. Had he been more perspicacious, New York might
today be a French-speaking city.

I walked up to the Place Sainte-Catherine to see the delightful
fifteenth-century church built by the shipbuilders of Honfleur to
give thanks for the final departure of the English. It is built entirely
of wood – what else would shipbuilders use? Inside it felt just like
being under an upturned boat, or rather a pair of boats side by
side. Then I walked out on the Deauville road; the Côte de Grace
was on one side of me, the estuary on the other. Here Baudelaire
wrote *L'Invitation au Voyage*, still beside the Seine.

In due course I came to the Ferme Saint-Siméon, once a country
inn, now a less modest hotel and restaurant. It was here that the
Impressionists gathered in their pre-Argenteuil days. Indeed, it
was here that it all started. It was here that Boudin persuaded the
young Havre artist Monet to give up caricatures, to look in
preference at landscape and clouds.

I sat on the terrace and looked at the view which had triggered
off the movement. It was a real Monet day today. The sun shone
through shifting sea-mists, putting a luminous blur over the river
and the sea. All I could see of Le Havre across the estuary was the
soft silver gleam of the oil tanks.

Honfleur still keeps its artistic connections. There was an exhibition of work by modern Honfleur artists on show, though I
noticed that many of the exhibitors were well-known Paris
names and their connection with Honfleur seemed a little
tenuous.

There are several galleries round the Vieux Bassin and I wandered into Katia Granoff's. I had met Madame Granoff in Paris
and I had not realized she had a gallery here too. She gave me a
book of her poems to read as she was at the moment on the telephone to New York, a thought which would have greatly surprised Champlain and Verrazano, and possibly even Monet. On
the wall facing me were three Monets, all of the Seine: a rosy
Rouen, a grey hill perhaps at Villequier and, best of all, a sunny
Vernon, the church, the hill, the river, all sunlight and sky and

water. It was not very large, perhaps I might buy it, I tempted myself. Keep it as a souvenir of my journey down the Seine. Pay for it out of my royalties.

'Is the middle one for sale?' I asked Madame Granoff. 'How much is it?'

'For you,' she whispered, covering the mouthpiece, 'I will let you have it for fourteen million old francs.'

Sadly I shook my head. 'I haven't got that amount with me in travellers cheques,' I explained.

23

I returned to Le Havre to catch the train, and this time I came to terms with the town. I ignored the new town, Perret's work, and instead I concentrated on the part which had given the town its name and reason for existence – the harbour. It was in these waters that had sprung that forest of masts during the American War of Independence, beside these quays that the ships had docked which carried the massive French aid for the rebel colonies. The transatlantic connection begun then continues today with such vast ships as the *France*, the *United States*, the *Rotterdam* and others who use Le Havre as their French port (the Queens remain faithful to Cherbourg).

Size – that is the great feature of the harbour. Big ships, enormous sheds full of huge trunks of mahogany and other tropical trees, the great dry dock like a canyon, the acres of water, the miles of sheds, the busy purposefulness of everything.

I also visited the Maison de la Culture. This is a recent building – it was only opened in 1961 – and it seems to belong to a different century from the rest of the new town. Its architect, Guy Lagneau, has built it largely of glass to reflect the changing colours of the sea and the sky. It has a lightness and a sense of proportion sadly missing in Perret's work. Standing outside the Maison on the seafront is a huge monumental sculpture by Adam, like a giant pencil point with a hole through it. I can imagine it causing some raised eyebrows among the solid Normans when it was first placed in position.

Inside, the Maison is excellently designed and lit. The pictures are hung on movable screens which can be altered to suit the needs of the current exhibition. The eye is never blurred by looking at two pictures at once, and you are led on, floating effortlessly, from one masterpiece to another.

I had gone to see the remarkable permanent collection and, in particular, after my visit to Honfleur, the Boudins. I must admit I was disappointed. Here were the first cloudscapes, the first glimmer of opalescence, but his colours were still sombre Barbizon colours, his preferred subjects deliberately murky – 'Storm over Le Havre', 'Dusk over the Bassin de Commerce'. Did he always stay indoors on sunny days? His palette, which has been framed and hung, has as its dominating colour brown.

I moved on to his greater disciples, Renoir, Manet, Sisley at Moret, Monet beside his ponds, Pissarro on the Quai de Southampton. It was a recapitulation of my journey.

The Maison has also a good collection of contemporary art; Manessier, Villon, Estève, Vuillard and, in particular, a splendid Walch 'Vol et Voile', a dizzy pattern of sails and seagulls. But the pride of the collection are the Dufys. Boudin may have had a brown sombre soul, but Dufy's was joyous Mediterranean blue. Whether he was painting the warm south or the chilly north, Nice or Le Havre, the hot sunlight was always there. 'Fête Maritime au Havre', 'La Plage et L'Estacade', 'Le Havre à l'Arc en Ciel', I moved in a jubilant world of regattas and sails and flags and, always above all, the deep blue Mediterranean sky. 'Yet do what I may,' he once wrote, 'I only give you a fraction of my inward joy.'

He was giving me plenty. I felt as exhilarated as if I had just had a Pernod.

I found other good things in Le Havre. The Forêt de Montgeon, for instance, where in the middle of the town you suddenly find yourself under a canopy of dense summer green. Or the lighthouse on top of the cliff at La Hève, with the fresh Channel breeze on my cheek, and the sea glinting like beaten metal, and the hilly

Norman coastline, all the way from Honfleur to Arromanches. It was more than twenty-one years since I had last seen it on a June morning, and even so it was clearer in my mind's eye than now through the August haze.

I went down to Sainte-Adresse, the 'Nice' of Le Havre, and there I found a bar, 'Le Week-End' where the gay young people of that rich quarter meet each other. Across the street was a restaurant with an open-air terrace. I sat there under a striped umbrella, looking across the estuary at the Côte de Grace, drinking an Alsace Riesling and eating big platefuls of fruits de mer: a large crab called a tourteau, shrimps, mussels, cockles, whelks, limpets. Below me in the bay a yacht race was just starting, white sails, coloured sails, burgees.

With a sudden sunburst of excitement I realized at last where I was. I was no longer in a Sisley or a Monet, or even in the Book of Hours. I was in a Dufy. And looking at the sky round the edge of my striped umbrella, bless me if it wasn't deep Mediterranean blue after all!

I went and sat on the beach. The *Rotterdam* was just leaving port and I watched her go. This, I estimated, was the end of the river, the exact point where it became the sea. It was almost exactly a year since I had stood at the source of the Seine and watched it bubbling out of the ground into Sequana's pool. Four hundred and eighty-five slow, winding miles, four seasons of the year, four fair provinces: Burgundy, Champagne, Île-de-France, Normandy; all the way from a lonely valley to a busy port. All the way too from palaeolithic man to nuclear man. Kings, saints, lovers, conquerors, painters, writers, sailors, architects, engineers, bishops, bargees, fishermen, cooks – they had all passed this way before me. For the Seine is many things: a waterway, a geographical feature, a religion, a landscape, a way of life, a history of France, a record of human achievement.

A year ago I had tossed a coin into Sequana's pool, and now at the end of my journey I threw a pebble into the sea.

Index